MARKED BY DESIGN

"The Passion of a Burning Heart"

JOHN BLONDO

FOREWORD BY MICHAEL DOW

ANNA —

Jesus is pleased with your obedience to His call — Praying for you —

JOHN

BURNING ONES

Marked by Design
by John Blondo

Printed in Canada

ISBN 978-0-9963641-0-2

Dedication

I dedicate this book to my bride, RainyDawn, whose unconditional love captivates my heart every breath of every day.

To my deeply loved sons, John Zinzendorf and Jeremiah Finney, who continually delight my heart. Our Father in heaven will fulfill every detail of His purpose for your lives.

To my covenant brother, Michael Dow, who led me to the burning heart of Jesus and stayed with me there. I honor and love you. Glory or Death!

Table of Contents

Foreword

By Michael Dow

God has a divine design, a protocol of heaven, by which He chooses to mold and make men into that which He needs to further the expansion of the Kingdom in their generation. This process is proven, tried, and true. Over the ages this faithful process has conformed many that have gone on to display the glory of God through their lives. Many have seen cities, regions, and nations shaken by the power of God. Many have been burning torches that have reflected the light of the Son in their day. Many have become a voice.

It is safe to say that for as many that have completely given themselves over to God, they have found that He knows what He is doing. He knows how to shape and to mold. He knows just the right process for each individual by which He has chosen. The Father knows there is much more that we may become, and He is excited to walk us through to this place, if we will absolve ourselves of the striving that is so encouraged and prevalent in our day.

There is a striving in our day to prove that we are better than the next. There is a striving to demonstrate that God has entrusted us with "the goods." A striving that causes men to desire recognition. A striving that creates processes and doorways into influence and platforms that were never God ordained or birthed.

There is a ministry culture in place in our day that teaches men how to lift themselves and introduce themselves to the world. There is a ministry culture that is well accepted in our day that applauds men who network harder and outperform the other guy for opportunities. What has become of us? We are to be known, regarded, according to the apostle Paul, as those who have been entrusted with the mysteries of God.[1]

The men and women that God is looking for cannot be purchased; they must be made. They cannot be purchased because they are not cheap imitations; they are originals. Originals that have not simply been photocopied into whatever the current trend is or the

---

[1] 2 Cor. 2:4, NASB

thing that is most accepted and palatable by the world in the moment. Men built not upon the world's formulas for success and increase, but fashioned by the hand of the Master for His divine purpose. These are men and women that have really encountered God, and by that encounter, have wholly given themselves over.

The men and women that God is looking for cannot be purchased because they are not cheap imitations; they are originals.

Ezekiel 9:4 gives us an interesting picture to consider. The Spirit of God catches up Ezekiel in a vision, and one of the many things God shows him are six angels being summoned to execute judgment on the people for their calloused hearts and unrepentant sin. Yet, in the midst of the angels that are being sent to execute judgment stands one, whom Ezekiel has seen in an earlier vision, that is directed to go throughout the people and mark those on their forehead who have been weeping and groaning according to the detestable acts being done amongst the people in the nation.[2] The one who is walking amongst the people to mark them is Jesus.

---

[2] Ezek. 9:4, NASB

One of the peculiar things about being marked on your forehead is that it would be very noticeable. It would be very noticeable to you, yet also to everyone else. Being marked on your forehead wouldn't leave a lot of wiggle room or give way to a place to hide. Being marked on your forehead would clearly distinguish you from the rest of the crowd. A mark on the forehead of this nature would let the rest know what you were all about, and most importantly, to whom you belonged. It would be a very clear determiner of having been selected, set apart.

We need men and women in our day that have really encountered the presence and the person of Jesus, and therefore have genuinely been transformed.

We need men and women in our day that have been marked by God. We need men and women in our day that have really encountered the presence and the person of Jesus, and therefore have genuinely been transformed. We need men and women who stand up as a voice only because they have first found their lives laid down at the feet of Jesus. We need men and women who have become overtaken by the Spirit of God!

For any and all that know John Blondo or have had the privilege to interact with him, you know one thing: John is a man that has been overtaken by the

Spirit of God. John is a man that has been marked by God. John lives the things he preaches. There is no disconnect between the man and the message that God has given to him to sound off in our day.

I encourage you to journey through these pages with the Holy Spirit. I also encourage you not to continue if you are simply looking for ministry gimmicks or tricks; they will not be found. This is not a text of that nature. There are no shortcuts described here. There are no magic formulas, no corners to be cut.

However, this is not a new call. In actuality this is one that has echoed throughout the ages. This is a call that many have discerned in their generation. This is a violent call to the total abandonment of self and the ways of the world. This is a call to fiery love and the lifelong pursuit and enjoyment of a person, Jesus the Son. This is a call by the Master that resounds in the hearts of men and women and says, "Come unto Me! Follow Me!" I pray you would allow the Holy Spirit to mark you for the glory of God as you encounter Jesus in the pages that follow.

Acknowledgments

Thank you to my exceptional dad, mom, and beautiful family for shaping my life.

I honor the leadership team of Bethlehem in New York City and the amazing church family I serve for standing with me.

My sincere gratitude to Pastor Lowell Perkins and the Jefferson City church family he leads for sixteen years of supernatural generosity.

Thanks to Jim McMahel for creating a unique and impacting cover design and to Kathy Curtis for your ministry in editing. You are transforming our world.

My profound love to Pastor Tim Shuttlesworth for opening his heart and home to me as a young preacher.

To the greatest band of brothers a man could ever have—I am honored to stand with you!

To Jesus—my Savior and my eternal song!

Introduction

⌒

Jesus marked your life. He set you apart for Himself. His heart is burning with intense desire for you personally. Every moment He is thinking about you and He burns with all-consuming affection for you. He placed unique gifting in you that would evoke pleasure in Him and uniquely reflect Him in your generation.

The incomprehensible reality is that the Sovereign Lord of all formed every part of you in the womb of your mother with the specific intent that you would desire Him. His unconditional love is aimed directly at your heart. His burning heart is fixed on you. He wants to immerse you in desire for Him and captivate your heart to be only satisfied in His presence. If you are striving to please Him, then you are still dead in religion. Let Him lead.

WE DANCE

You steady me
Slow and sweet, we sway
Take the lead and I will follow
Finally ready now
To close my eyes and just believe
That You won't lead me where You don't go

When my faith gets tired
And my hope seems lost
You spin me round and round
And remind me of that song
The one You wrote for me
And we dance

And I've been told
To pick up my sword
And fight for love
Little did I know
That Love had won for me
Here in Your arms

You still my heart again
And I breathe You in
Like I've never breathed 'till now

And I will lock eyes
With the One who's ransomed me
The One who gave me joy for mourning
And I will lock eyes
With the One who's chosen me
The One who set my feet to dancing

I invite you to run with me into the arms of Jesus. Lean back. Press your head against the heart of the greatest lover one can ever know. Listen to His pulsating heart. Embrace the rhythm of unfailing love. Surrender. Absolute surrender.

You are going to hear the original song He sings over you. Lock eyes. Listen to His voice sing melodies written only for you. Tune your ears to harmonies direct from His throne. Dance. Pour your deepest longings into Him! Jesus is revealing Himself to you, as you have never encountered before. You are marked by design!

1

Vision

Jesus, Thy blood and righteousness
My beauties are, my glorious dress,
'Midst flaming worlds, in these arrayed
With joy shall I lift up my head.
—Zinzendorf [3]

The vision is Jesus. The time is now. The future is yours. You have opened this book because Jesus wants to know you. He set you up. You are encountering Him right now in this text. His unconditional, perfect, intense, unfailing, supernatural love is yours as you open your heart to Him. Look at Him!

---

[3] Nikolaus Ludwig von Zinzendorf, "Jesus, Thy Blood and Righteousness," *cyberhymnal.org*, http://cyberhymnal.org/htm/j/t/jtbloodr.htm.

There is a secret place. Close the door behind you. Open your eyes. You have access to His throne room. You can go inside the veil. You have to be honest about who you are and where you come from with Him. No hiding. No pretense. Come just as you are. Nothing you can do grants access. Jesus is calling you to union with Himself.

There is a secret place. Close the door behind you. Open your eyes. You have access to His throne room. Come just as you are. Jesus is calling you to union with Himself.

God will give you a city. He will give you a region. The Lord of the Harvest will give you a nation. He is calling a woman. He is calling a man that He can give an entire continent to as their inheritance. With God *all* things are possible! The Holy Spirit is marking you right now with a vision of Jesus. When you adore Him, you will race into the dark places and be with Jesus there.

Rescue! Risk! Spill your blood. He spilled His blood for you. Lay your life down. Jesus laid His life down for you. Now is your moment. You are marked by design. Love the oppressed. Love the oppressor. In Jesus' name, *love!*

Experience the passion of His burning heart. You are marked—identifiable by intent. Distinct.

Pronounced. Striking. Clear. Manifest. Evident. The Father is revealing Himself to you. Jesus is writing history through your life.

Abandon everything to God. Do whatever it takes to be so completely broken before Him that God Himself possesses you. Jesus is worthy. That's the vision. He is worthy of absolute adoration. Burn for *Him* alone. Let Him breathe on you. Breathe the atmosphere of eternity now.

You are the message. God is releasing your unique destiny. You are becoming the Gospel. He invites you to be marked by His presence. You are going to see Jesus. Love Him without limits. Hold nothing back. When you see Him face to face there will be no regrets.

> **Do whatever it takes to be so completely broken before Him that God Himself possesses you. Jesus is worthy. That's the vision.**

I am obsessed with Jesus. Come with me! Follow Him. Gaze on Him alone. Live in the constant awareness of an audience of one. Give Him your deepest affections, your all. Every breath! We are the new breed of laid-down lovers. We are apostles marked by design. Miracles. Favor. Open doors. Nothing is more beautiful than Jesus Himself. He is my greatest treasure. *He is my vision!*

Why were you born? God Himself spoke to a young Israeli: "I formed you in the womb. I knew you before you were born. I set you apart. I appointed you a prophet to the nations."[4] There is a clear, specific reason God formed you. Listen to the word He is speaking over your life.

His voice consumes and His voice calls. When God speaks, no power can stop His Word. You didn't come into this world before your time. You are here in season.

God declares to Jeremiah: "I am watching over my Word to perform it."[5] God Himself watches to see that every word He speaks is fulfilled. He personally will make *every* word He gives you come true.

God, the Eternal Word, the Incarnate Word, the Creative Word, the Living Word is speaking. The voice of the Lord creates, convicts, and cleanses. His voice consumes and His voice calls. When God speaks, no power can stop His Word. You didn't come into this world before your time. You are here in season.

When Joseph's brothers saw him in the distance they scornfully mocked, "Here comes that dreamer!" They arrogantly believed they had the power to stop the dream. You can't stop the vision. You can't stop

---

[4] Jer. 1:5
[5] Jer. 1:12

God's Word. Those very same brothers bowed down before the powerful Egyptian ruler they didn't even know was their brother. God watches over His Word to fulfill it.

Jeremiah is clear. The word of the Lord came personally to Him. Impacted by his father serving in priestly ministry and the revival under Josiah, Jeremiah encountered God personally. He must be your personal vision.

God will tell you where to go and you will go there. He will tell you what to say and you will declare it. The greatest vision is God Himself. In forty years of ministry, Jeremiah experienced brutal rejection and searing pain. When your vision is Jesus, He stands up in you. Jesus will make you this man of vision and expectation.

Leonard Ravenhill graphically calls out this man: "He is accepted by God and totally rejected by men. He sets up that which is upset. He calls in line those who are out of line. He has no price tags. He breathes the rarefied air of inspiration. He lives in splendid isolation. He is excommunicated while alive and exalted when dead. He announces, pronounces, and denounces. God talks to him about men and he talks to men about God. He is ordained by God and disdained by men.

"He hides with God in the secret place but has nothing to hide in the marketplace. He is considered too austere, too committed. He comes daily from the throne room of a holy God. He cries with a voice this century has not heard because he has seen a vision no man in this century has seen."[6] God is calling you to Himself—to this vision!

FIRST ENCOUNTER
WITH THE HOLY SPIRIT

I am just an ordinary person. Born and raised in New York City, my early childhood years were filled with love and a strong desire for Jesus. My maternal grandmother was sent home from the hospital at the age of thirty. The doctors informed my grandfather there was no medical procedure that could save her life.

At the time, my grandfather was not a Christ follower. My grandmother had a vision of her three small children (my mom, aunt, and uncle) and the enemy standing over them laughing. He told her: "You are going to die and these children will not be raised to serve God."

My grandma Lucia had extraordinary faith in God. She would lift herself up, leaning on a broom, and stand in her kitchen declaring that the blood of Jesus

---

[6] Leonard Ravenhill, "Picture of a Prophet," *Ravenhill,* http://www.ravenhill.org/prophet.htm.

healed her. After falling to the ground, she would pull herself up and make her declaration all over again. This continued over a period of days until Jesus supernaturally healed her.

Her life was marked by intense love for Jesus and her family. She lived in the secret place with God. The future of our family was transformed. She lived to see her children, grandchildren, and great grandchildren grow up. Every one of us is impacted by her love for Jesus. She wrote a personal letter to me every week over the years I was in Bible school and the many years in ministry throughout the nations of the world until she went to be with Jesus face to face.

I have never known a moment in my life when I did not know the intense love of Jesus for me.

My dad was consistently in the Word. My mom led us in prayer for missionaries around the world before my brothers, sister, and I would leave for school. Birthdays were special days when we would all gather on my parents' bed and begin the day together. I have never known a moment in my life when I did not know the intense love of Jesus for me.

At the age of seven, the Holy Spirit came to me in a unique way. I remember His coming as if it were today. It was Sunday night during the Christmas season.

Each class of children was walking into the sanctuary to begin our presentation to honor the coming of Jesus into our world. The atmosphere was charged. Everyone was singing "O Come All Ye Faithful."

As my feet were walking down that center aisle, listening to the adoration of Jesus, the Holy Spirit enveloped me and remained on me. I knew it was Him. What a sacred moment, beyond what words can describe. I treasure His presence more than my life itself.

The brilliance of the light of His presence birthed an overwhelming sense of awe and wonder within me. His presence lured me and loved me like I had never been loved before.

The church built a new sanctuary soon after that. One Sunday evening, I was taken up in a vision, standing right in front of the altar area. I was startled at first. Although completely aware that I was still standing inside the church, I was also in the throne room of God.

The brilliance of the light of His presence birthed an overwhelming sense of awe and wonder within me. I never wanted to leave that glory. His presence lured me and loved me like I had never been loved before.

At the age of eleven, my parents sacrificed so I could attend a camp led by German Pentecostals in

Brant Lake, New York. What a glorious and unique place! The boys my age went for two weeks during August. Brant Lake, in upstate New York, was vastly different than the Brooklyn I had known my whole life.

During those two weeks we had worship encounters every morning and evening. The subject was the presence of God manifested in the tabernacle built in the wilderness by the people of Israel. They had a model of the tabernacle and each session the leaders brought insights from God's Word into how to move deeper in His presence.

There was a stone fireplace in that room. Above the mantle were written the words: *Holiness unto the Lord.* These were the words God commanded to be inscribed on a gold plate and tied to the turban of the high priest. Aaron would feel the impact of that sacred diadem whenever he ministered.

One evening while seeking God with my face buried in those stones, I encountered the Holy Spirit in a way that transformed my life forever. You may say, "You were only eleven. What could you have known or understood of Him?"

I assure you, He came. He immersed me in Jesus Himself. I have no idea how long I was kneeling there. I do know He marked my life forever in that encounter. There is no one more precious to me than Jesus. I am in love with Him and He is in love with me.

Many years later as a cross-cultural ambassador living in China, I returned to New York to preach. I was driving to a church in upstate New York when I realized I was close to Brant Lake. I followed the narrow road until I reached the entryway into Pilgrim Camp.

It was October so the season for camp was long past. I parked my car and walked up the road into the area where that meeting with God took place so many years ago. A young man who was caretaker for the property pulled up in a pickup truck and asked who I was. I told him about my life and ministry in China and that I had attended camp here as a boy.

There is no one more precious to me than Jesus. I am in love with Him and He is in love with me.

My tears can't be stopped even now as I remember how that man unlocked the doors to that holy place and I walked inside. I went over to the exact place at that stone altar where the Holy Spirit met with me and Jesus immersed me in Himself.

Before I ever heard the mandate to go to the nations, He lavished on me a *vision of Himself*. He drew me to Himself. There is no greater wonder. There is no greater love. There is no greater vision. There is no greater calling than to be with Him, to live within the veil, to live in the secret place with God.

YOUR YOUNG MEN SHALL SEE VISIONS

At the age of sixteen, I left my life in New York City to begin training for ministry in Rhode Island. A missionary from South America founded Zion Bible College. No room, board, or tuition was charged. It was designed as a place to train Spirit-filled ministers who could not afford to attend college. Founded as the School of the Prophets, it was a place of daily provision and especially marked by the strong presence of God.

The president of the college was also the pastor of the church all of the students attended. Sunday morning and Sunday evening we gathered to worship. Monday evening was the church prayer meeting. Tuesday night was men's devotions. Wednesday we gathered at night for expository Bible study. Thursday was set aside for praying for the nations of the world. Monday through Friday we

There is no greater vision. There is no greater calling than to be with Him, to live within the veil, to live in the secret place with God.

had powerful chapel services right before lunch. Many days, students continued praying and never ate lunch.

I am so thankful to God for directing my steps to this center of vision and sacrifice. In the church sanctuary, there is a huge painted mural that covers the entire front wall. On the left is an open Bible. In the center, the artist painted a cross and crown of thorns.

When He is our vision, His heart for the nations will be revealed to us.

On the right, the cup of sacrifice.

During my very first semester, standing in this sanctuary, the Holy Spirit came. The regular college class schedule was canceled. We experienced God for hours at those altars night after night. No one wanted to leave. We were taken up in Him!

To this day I have never met anyone who had an identical experience to that which I am about to describe. I had never read of such an experience. Quite honestly, I rarely speak of it. It is beyond the vocabulary of any earthly language.

As the front altar area was packed with students seeking God, I stood up. My eyes were closed. I could hear sounds of those around me; however, in my spirit Jesus took me to the nations of the world. I saw the faces of the people clearly. It was just as if I was watching it on a screen, only better. I was actually there!

As I opened my mouth, I was speaking in tongues. My mind knew fully and completely the meaning of every word I was speaking. I saw specific gatherings of people and I began to preach full messages in tongues. My mind understood in English what I was preaching, yet what was audible to those around me in that room were languages from heaven.

For literal hours, I stood and preached on multiple nights carried by the Spirit into the nations. Oh how precious the prophetic demonstrations of the Lord! When He is our vision, His heart for the nations will be revealed to us.

As that move of God continued for weeks, we gathered in many places across the campus. One afternoon in the lower chapel of the church, I began to type as directed by the Spirit. I saw myself seated at a desk on the mission field and I began to type messages given by the Lord. The Sovereign Lord, who knows the end from the beginning, reveals that future to His servants. Oh how strange it must have looked to those who despise the things of God. How beautiful to the Father to see His sons and daughters immersed in Him!

He took me into heaven.

The main focus of His heart is not what we do for Him. His desire is that we will come to Him and desire Him more than anyone or anything.

He allowed me to witness the torment of hell. No mortal can ever be the same. He desires that we have a greater revelation of Him. He wants us to love Him completely. This love will take us to the nations!

LIVING THE DREAM

As God reveals Himself to us, His desire is that our hearts remain humble before Him. The main focus of His heart is *not* what we do for Him. His desire is that we will come to Him and desire Him more than anyone or anything.

God opposes the proud but gives grace to the humble.[7] King David was walking around on the roof of his palace when he saw a woman bathing and gave in to the lust in his heart. Running for his life in the wilderness, he was totally dependent on God. With his armies engaged in fierce battle, he was walking on the roof and living in luxury when he fell.

Nebuchadnezzar, the young dictator, was in his palace, content and prosperous. God had warned him in mercy; however, the heart of this king was not responsive. As he was walking on the roof of his royal palace, he credits all of the majesty that he sees before him to his own power and for his own glory.

No matter how high you stand in this world, God is enthroned so much higher than where you stand. While the words were still on Nebuchadnezzar's lips, a voice from heaven spoke and his royal authority was immediately removed. The proud king, now insane, lived with the wild animals for a period of seven years.

---

[7] James 4:6

The vision is Jesus. The vision is not about you. It is not about the fame of your name or the extent of your influence in the world. God empowers the humble. He walks closely with those who adore Him and recognize that it is all for His name. As God reveals Himself to you, stay *seated*. Don't walk around on the roof like David and Nebuchadnezzar. He is King. You are seated with Christ in heavenly places. He has marked you to love Him, to be His. He created you to accomplish a specific purpose. Live in His power. You will not fall. Don't walk around on the high places in pride. By the power of the Holy Spirit, stay seated with Christ!

God showed me in a vision that I would be preaching at my graduation from Bible college. At age nineteen, that vision became reality and I stood to preach in front of a packed church in East Providence, Rhode Island.

The message God gave me was "The Necessity of a Radical in This Age of the Reasonable." The depth of man's need continually calls to the depth of God's fullness. Our world needs leaders who have had deep

The vision is Jesus. The vision is not about you. God empowers the humble. He walks closely with those who adore Him and recognize that it is all for His name.

experiences with God and demonstrate the way to truth and salvation in Jesus.

Jeremiah was asked if there was a word from the Lord. We are the message. We demonstrate the word of the Lord in a world destitute of deep experiences with God. In the midst of violent winds and imminent destruction, Paul declares: "I believe God. It will happen just as He told me."[8] This word marked my life eternally. I cannot speak until I have seen.

Seeing the invisible and choosing to fix our gaze on Him is what liberates our voice to speak freedom and to declare the mind of Christ to those who are bleeding all around us.

John the Baptizer gazed on Jesus. It was that seeing that released him to tell the multitudes to look and see the Lamb of God who takes away all sin. Seeing the invisible and choosing to fix our gaze on Him is what liberates our voice to speak freedom and to declare the mind of Christ to those who are bleeding all around us. We need more than analysis. We need authority.

Hear the Word of the Lord! Abraham declared that God would provide. Caleb said: Give me this mountain. I am able to drive out every enemy *just as the Lord*

---

[8] Acts 27:25

told me. David, facing his giant, boldly told him that his covenant God would certainly deliver him from his hand that very day.

Our world has yet to see what God will do with one man, one woman totally dedicated to Him. God will turn your mountains of severe sorrow into monuments of spiritual success. The Word of the Lord is sure!

The message burns within me stronger today than when I delivered these words so many years ago as a teenager. God immediately began to bring the vision into reality.

That summer immediately after graduation, students from Zion traveled as a team to Sicily. I had the privilege of preaching overseas for the first time. The visions of my freshmen year were now actual ministry experiences and I was preaching the actual messages first preached as a prophetic demonstration.

The voice you choose to believe always determines the future you experience.

The voice you choose to believe always determines the future you experience. Fear is a liar. I choose to believe the Word of the Lord. His Word is within me like *fire*...burning, ever burning with passion for Him. I choose to set my mind on things above—not on earthly, temporal things. I am raised with Christ and I choose to live in that eternal reality.

ONE NIGHT AND ONE HUNDRED YEARS

Reinhard Bonnke was told during the early years of his ministry in Africa that he must follow the well-tried and proven methods of that denominational organization. He had no rest until he obeyed the voice of the Spirit of God. Choosing to follow the voice of the Lord, he saw more people come to Jesus for salvation in one night than that whole African mission saw in one hundred years. As of this writing, Christ for All Nations has documented over 73 million decisions for Jesus. Whose voice are you going to believe? Join us in this new breed of radicals obsessed with a burning vision of Jesus. Only He is worthy of your gaze!

The journey continues. While ministering in Zambia and Zimbabwe, God spoke a powerful word over my life. He said He goes before me and is preparing the way. Two pastors from Mozambique took my picture and told me they would be praying every day for me personally and the ministry God has called me to in China. Soon after this word, I packed two suitcases and departed from John F. Kennedy airport in New York City for a new life in Shanghai, China.

There are no words to describe my emotions as I looked out of the window of the plane and my natural eyes saw mainland China for the first time. When I arrived in Shanghai, I knew only how to say "thank you" and "hello" in Mandarin. I had a phone number for a Chinese language school. That's how I began.

That evening in 1993, I jumped into a taxi and said the name of a hotel. The driver nodded and we made our way through the intense traffic of the most populated city in the most populated nation of the world. It was dark. The burning light of Jesus now invaded this darkness! I called the language school the next day, secured housing on the sixth floor of a very simple building, and began to live the dream of seeing Jesus reveal Himself to those who have never heard His name before.

God was with us. We planted an international church in Shanghai. Miracles of provision marked our life day by day. Doors opened for ministry throughout Asia. We traveled to Mongolia. The nation only had a handful of Christ followers. After three days, a new church was planted with over six hundred in attendance. Hope Church quickly grew to over a thousand. The deaf were healed. A woman one hundred years old responded to the Gospel the very first time she heard it in her life. There was exuberant rejoicing and dancing as breakthrough came to a nation. A Bible training center was opened immediately.

Our church plant in Shanghai gave 100 percent of our first offering on the first Sunday we gathered for this Bible school in Mongolia. We continued to give the entire first Sunday offering every month to missions and apostolic church planting. We outgrew three facilities within seventeen months. I had the amazing honor of preaching at a conference of university students from thirty-four different nations who were all gathered in Shanghai.

Young adults from Albania, Romania, France, Indonesia, Japan, Australia, Rwanda, Madagascar, São Tomé and Príncipe, Chad, and many others were rocked by God's presence as He moved powerfully in our lives. We participated in water baptisms of national Chinese believers who risked their lives to declare their allegiance to Jesus. We were part of a network that delivered Bibles to leaders who had never held God's Word in their own hands.

We were living the book of Acts. The voice of the Holy Spirit was continual and specific. The vision is Jesus! We traveled in Pune, India where the deaf, blind, crippled, and mute were all set free. A four-year-old boy spoke for the first time. A vision of Jesus directed a man to the meetings and he heard the Gospel of the Kingdom for the first time and was radically transformed.

Many who were demon possessed were delivered. Miracles of salvation were astounding. In Lucknow, in northern India, a doctor from Hong Kong prayed for a lady with a huge tumor that was instantly healed.

Over one thousand people made decisions for Jesus in those encounters.

Sunday, October 3, 1994 I stood with more than one million people in an outdoor plaza in Seoul, South Korea for a powerful prayer meeting. Delegates from 134 nations gathered. I was thrilled to be with the Chinese from mainland China. A choir of two thousand lifted their voices and the glory of God filled our lives.

God has allowed me to stand in Alexanderplatz in the former East Germany and preach outdoors. There are no more parades of communist youth there. We were there preaching the power of the Living Christ! Our team stayed in the former headquarters of the dreaded East German secret police. Candles and prayer proved more powerful than machine guns and dictators.

God raised up partners to join us from all over the world. Excited teens marched in a parade of nations in a church of four thousand in Barbados. As I ministered there, God joined our hearts together. We were given a miraculous offering of thousands of US dollars from a church in Hong Kong that had been praying for God to send someone into Shanghai to pioneer a church.

NOT FOR SALE!

God has protected my life through multiple earthquakes and continual dangers. One of those earthquakes was the most severe in the recorded history of that nation. There is a price to pay when God marks your life. The enemy will try to steal your God-given vision from you. He will try to get you to sell out, take an easier path, keep the waters calm, to not be so radical.

I knew I was a marked man early on. Sitting in a McDonald's in West Virginia in the beginning years of our ministry, a young man walked in and called to me. He wanted me to come outside. A voice told him to grab me and beat the life out of me. That morning he had dedicated his life as a high priest to Satan. He had never seen me before that moment. In the natural, he knew nothing about me. God protected me. The impact stayed with me. This is war! Jesus is real. His call is real. The powers of darkness are real. We overcome every day in Jesus' name. Never compromise. Never back down. Never give in to fear.

There is a price to pay when God marks your life. The enemy will try to steal your God-given vision from you.

He had everything he could ever want. The golden tapestries in his palace were the best money could buy. The carved designs in the doors, the costly marble floors, and the abundance of food filled his opulent palace. Yet all of his servants and his entire splendor couldn't satisfy this king. There was something he still wanted...a vineyard.

It was close to his royal residence. He could see it every day. He wanted it. He coveted it. There was only one problem. It was not for sale. Not at any price!

Not that this king hadn't tried. He offered the owner an exchange. He promised him an even better vineyard…larger, a better view. He offered money. Your enemy is in the business of making deals. Business proposals with unbelievers are his specialty.

Pharaoh told Moses he could go but the flocks and herds had to be left behind. Moses boldly confronted him and declared not one hoof would remain.

Judas sold out for thirty pieces of silver. He sold himself and will experience the torture of that decision for eternity.

Naboth was a different breed. He marched to the beat of a different drummer. You couldn't buy him. He knew the God of the covenant.

This is war! Jesus is real. His call is real. The powers of darkness are real. We overcome every day in Jesus' name. Never compromise. Never back down. Never give in to fear.

Naboth knew that God had spoken. The land was never to be permanently sold because it belonged to God. This man is extraordinary because he understood that God is the owner and he wasn't about to give up the inheritance of his fathers to an earthly king.

Ahab runs home to his palace…pouting, sullen, sulking. His wife steps in when he refuses to eat. They conspire to murder. They lie. Naboth is executed outside the city.

There is a cost when you obey the vision. Loving Jesus with all of your heart will cost you everything.

There is a cost when you obey the vision. Loving Jesus with all of your heart will cost you everything. Living in fulfillment of your destiny always means confronting the Ahabs and Jezebels. Their words sting. Their lies are believed. Blood flows.

It's not good to overemphasize the need overseas, they say. Your enemy will try to silence your voice. He may execute you. He can never silence you. Your blood still speaks. The word of the Lord comes to Elijah and he confronts Ahab.

WHAT YOU COMPROMISE TO GET— YOU WILL LOSE

The man of God tells him he has *sold himself* to do evil in the eyes of the Lord. Ahab and Jezebel pay for their compromise with their lives. I will never compromise that Christ's blood is the only way into a right relationship with God. You cannot follow Jesus if you will not deny yourself.

I will never compromise that Christ's mandate is the personal responsibility of every Christ follower.

His mandate is not negotiable. This generation must reach this generation!

I will never compromise that a supernatural assignment can only be accomplished by supernatural power. Wait in the city until you are endued with power. Without Jesus, **This generation must reach this generation!** you can do *nothing*. Be continually immersed in the Holy Spirit. Invade the nations with the love of Jesus. You are not for sale. You are marked by vision. The vision is Jesus.

2

Desperation

"Young man, I say to you, get up!"
—Jesus (Luke 7:14)

Death stings. You were born into a war. There is a confrontation at the city gate day after day for the eternal destiny of every man and every woman breathing. Cries of desperation fill the air.

She had recently buried her husband. In that moment, she had the strength of her son's embrace. Her only son stood at her side and walked with her as they lovingly placed his body in the ground.

Today, how could she go on? The tears pour down her cheeks. Her heart is shattered. Every tomorrow seems dark. The pain is searing. The large crowd with her attempts to console her. The words seem empty, shallow, hollow. Her only son is dead. His shrouded body is being carried out of the town gate.

Then, everything changes. Love is about to confront death face to face. The supernatural love of God, that furious, relentless, pursuing love is coming toward her.

He is not a distant God. He hears your cry. He sees into your deepest longing. He is unafraid of defilement. He does not fear death.

Jesus is the exact representation of His Father in heaven. Following the specific directive of His Father, Jesus approaches the town of Nain surrounded by His disciples and a large crowd. Nazareth is only a few miles away. Jesus personally knew these roads. Today, breakthrough was imminent at this town gate.

Jesus is walking in *this* region. When He walks in everything changes. He comes to the brokenhearted. He walks toward your crushed and wounded heart. You feel ripped, torn apart. You are without hope. Death has invaded your heart. Darkness has swallowed up your hope. No appetite. Your only song is the lament of what used to be. No idea where to turn. Nothing makes sense. You are the walking wounded headed to the burial of all of your dreams. Look up!

Jesus is walking toward you. In your desperation, He comes and breathes on you.

The author of life comes to you. You were not even thinking about Him yet His thoughts are focused on you. Your mind could not even embrace a God so loving, so powerful, so intimate, yet He is now standing right in front of you!

"As he approached the town gate, a dead person was being carried out—the only son of his mother, and she was a widow. And a large crowd from the town was with her. When the Lord saw her, his heart went out to her and he said, 'Don't cry.' Then he went up and touched the coffin, and those carrying it stood still."[9]

We know Jesus called out to her while still a distance away. His intense love for her was immediate, "Don't cry." When He saw the weeping, His heart is one with hers. He is coming ever closer until he touches the coffin. He knew the heart of the Father toward her. He has the authority to remove the cause of these tears. Jesus is present. All of Him is present in her most desperate moment.

Jesus approaches her. Jesus calls to her before she calls to Him. Jesus comes near. He is not a distant God. He hears your cry. He sees into your deepest

---

[9] Luke 7:12-14

longing. He is unafraid of defilement. He does not fear death.

The touch of Jesus stops the movement. Their path is set. This young man's body is on a one-way journey to the place of burial. The hand of Jesus literally stops the movement of these pallbearers. Luke specifically writes that those carrying the body stood still.

STILLNESS

His touch is designed to bring you into stillness. Be still, and know the I am.[10] Sudden attacks. External storms. Internal storms. Surrounded. Tight places. In the midst of desperate crisis, you can only experience God in stillness. So many voices are calling you. You have your agenda. It's all planned out. Receive

You can only experience God in stillness. Receive His touch. Let it all go. Be still. Stay in His presence.

His touch. Let it all go. Stop moving. Be still. Stay in His presence.

He will be exalted in every nation. He is with us. The God of Jacob is our fortress.[11] Jacob, the deceiver, has to be pinned to the ground to be born anew as Israel. God marks you with a new name and you

---

[10] Psalm 46:10, actual Hebrew translation
[11] Psalm 46:11

violently pursue Him *only* when you have experienced Him in stillness and continue to live in continual surrender and abandonment to *Him!*

The *voice of Jesus* can *only* be heard when you come to a place of stillness and abide there. Stop the rushing. Martha—sit down! Jesus is here! No one, nothing is more **If you ignore Him and keep going, you rush past your miracle. He is your life. He is the miracle.** important than His presence. If you ignore Him and keep going, you rush past your miracle. *He* is your life. He is the miracle.

Jesus then speaks to the dead man. In that stillness, Jesus said, "'Young man, I say to you, get up!' The dead man sat up and began to talk, and Jesus gave him back to his mother. They were all filled with awe and praised God...God has come to help his people.'"[12] The voice of Jesus cancels death. The voice of Jesus restores. The voice of Jesus gives back what was ripped from you. The voice of Jesus will fill *your* voice with awe and praise.

What amazing words that resurrected young man spoke! God raises *you* from the dead and *opens your mouth.* In the stillness, listen! His voice is calling to you,

---

[12] Luke 7:14-18

49

"Young man, I say to you, get up!" Our God speaks to those dead in their sin and commands life! Our God speaks to those whose dreams have long ago died and breathes on you with resurrection life. Listen! He is speaking to you right now!

GETTING BACK YOUR FIGHT

God marked your life. God's hand is on you. Reading this stirs His gift inside of you. You want to believe! You want to risk. You want to look up and see Jesus coming toward you. The worries, the pressures, the criticism, the false promises all stand as demonic warriors blocking your pathway. Deep inside, you know it's not too late.

God fulfills His promises. His heart toward you is good. He will fulfill His purpose for you—every detail. All of your dignity, your reputation, and your status—let it go! Break it and lay it at the feet of Jesus. Run to Him. Run into His arms.

David knew desperation. "You hem me in behind and before; you have laid your hand upon me."[13] The Hebrew verb here is unique in all of the psalms. God's hand surrounds me. God's hand forms me as a potter with clay. His hand hems me in—surrounded by favor. His hand hems me in—formed and designed uniquely by my Father!

---

[13] Psalm 139:5

The potter forming the clay with his hands is an art requiring prodigious skill. This is a science of sensitive hands in contrast to cheap, commercial, mass manufacturing. The Lord Himself places His hands on you. Jesus, filled with compassion, touched the man scarred by leprosy.

Our God speaks to those whose dreams have long ago died and breathes on you with resurrection life.

He spoke and the man was clean. Jesus took a twelve-year-old girl by the hand and life immediately came back into her body. His hands overturned the tables of the money changers, poured water into a basin to wash the feet of His disciples, and took five loaves of bread and two fish and men, women, and children feasted!

Those same hands lifted the bread and cup and inaugurated a new covenant. The hands of God were pierced with Roman spikes. Your name is engraved on the palms of those hands. These hands are forming you, marking you forever.

MASTER POTTER'S STUDIO

Today God is taking you to the Potter's house. Standing in the Master Potter's studio, you encounter the dazzling confluence of sovereignty and salvation, passion and perfection.

God selects us from unlikely places. He takes men from the gutters of brokenness and hopelessness. He reaches up to the lofty heights of arrogance and self-importance. He decrees what you will become. "I will make you to become what you cannot become by your own effort." In our desperation, we try to escape this process. This is the ceramic process of our life!

The Potter begins with the *crushing*. Rough clay is reduced under heavy pressure to liquid. Clay has to pour. We are pushed, crowded, struck, hit, and stepped on. God desires to pour out your life. Paul says to his son Timothy that he is being poured out like a drink offering. God's hand hemmed me in and His hand is still on me. The process continues over our lifetime.

You are now set up for *purifying*. The cream is poured through a screen to remove the impurities and imperfections. Things that are dear to you are falling off and are scooped away. Excesses. Insults. Slander. Complexities. The Master Potter wants *pure* devotion to Christ. He continues until we cry out: "God, all I want is *You!*"

Flint is now sprinkled in and the *firming* process commences. Substance is added to bring firmness. You thought you were going to fall apart. The prophetic Word comes in the night and begins to strengthen you, empower you, and build you. You have died and the life of Christ is being formed in you. His resolve fills your inner man. He is your strength!

The Potter will now begin the process of *wedging*. These are not hammer-like blows. These are squeezes. The moisture that builds up has to be pressed out. *Tears!* Pressing is done with consistency. Forty to fifty kneading motions are necessary for a six-pound piece. God is with you. He is not going to fail you. You thought

God determines how He wants to use you! It's not your call. You don't choose the design. His hands are holding you, centering you in Himself.

you would never go through anything like that again. Desperation. The vision is for an appointed time. Tears endure for the night. Joy is coming. Keep believing. Morning is coming!

Centering and shaping begin. The Potter must firmly secure the clay to the wheel head. Centering. Opening the clay. Pulling the clay to the shape the Potter desires and designs. *God determines how He wants to use you!* You understand that, don't you? It's not your call. You don't choose the design. His hands are holding you, centering you in Himself. Oh the beauty of His heart toward us! The strength of His hands! Sovereign hands holding you firmly. He will never let you go. You can count on that!

Now you think...*I'm ready. It's time.* To your shock, you are placed in a dank cellar of solitude. *Waiting.* Placed on a lonely shelf in a dark basement corner you mourn the loss of all the activity that once marked your identity. Cut off. Alone. You are there to dry, slowly, evenly. No song in your heart. The Potter leaves you there until the texture is right. *Refined!* God will open the door when it is time. Though the vision tarries, wait for it. It will certainly come and will not delay!

The Lord has laid His hand on you to form you into the image of Jesus. You are the message!

Sandpaper is used for *trimming*. You have to trim at the right stage of drying. The Master Craftsman has to use the right tools. Specially cut, reinforced smaller pieces are used which are perfect for smoothing over the rough edges. The Potter will strike one piece of textured clay against another to make it pliable in *His* hands. Iron will strike iron. There are clashes of disposition. This is the process of molding a life.

Finally, there is the *beautifying*. The glaze and the fire. The Lord has laid His hand on you to form you into the image of Jesus. *You are the message!* The hand of Jesus is on you. He commissions you to charge into the battle. He is sending you to the city gate. Go to the place of authority and proclaim the rule of God. Heal the sick. *Raise the dead!*

WARRIOR'S SONG

Listen to the words of this song written by an eyewitness. It is recorded in the book of warriors. These judges changed nations as they led the people of God directly into warfare.

"When the locks of hair grow long,
They let it blow wild in the wind.
The people volunteered with abandon,
bless God!
To God, yes to God, I'll sing!
God, when You marched across the
Fields of Edom, the earth quaked."[14]

Powerful lyrics written to God honoring Him for what *He* has accomplished. Warriors with long hair blowing wildly gallop with abandon into the battle. They never look back. Soldiers leaving their hair uncut in dedication. Their vow to God strong. God marches across the fields. The earth is quaking. God has *formed* your life to engage in a holy fight. Be ready to sacrifice!

You have to fight to make time for God in your life. You have to fight to sit with Him in the secret

---

[14] Judges 5:2-5, *The Message*

place for hours. You have to overcome challenges to have a great relationship with your wife. You have to be determined and violent in your pursuit of your God-given destiny.

The God of the covenant comes to Joseph when he is seventeen years old. In the darkness of night, he sees dreams that declare his destiny. This God who speaks downloads His dream into our spirit. Joseph sees his brothers bowing down to him. He sees the authority that God has promised him. He is obedient to His father and lives in the approval and blessing of his father.

Jealous brothers strip him of the long-sleeved robe of favor. False brothers will try to strip you of your Father's favor. They will sell you out. What did they buy with the silver they received for their betrayal of their brother? It could never silence the guilt that tormented their minds for over twenty years. Joseph is taken down to Egypt. To save nations, you will be taken down. To be the expression of Jesus on this earth, you must yield to this process.

Joseph knew God was with him down in Egypt. God was with Him in the prison dungeon. God's word is trustworthy! In desperation, Joseph pleads to be remembered. People you help will forget you. Your Father in heaven never forgets. In the exact timing of God, Joseph is exalted. Freshly shaved and wearing new garments, he enters the throne room of Pharaoh. God uses Joseph for the salvation of many nations. Thousands of lives are saved because Joseph stands and fights. Locked in prison, chained in darkness, He believes God!

Boldness, confidence, audacity, and authority are all birthed in the man willing to be taken down. This generation will be transformed as you yield to God's process in your life and you fight. Your revelation of Jesus will increase as you follow Him to the darkest places. He will *never* lead you where He does not go. He is in front! "Charge! This very day God has given you victory…isn't God marching before you?"[15] God commands you to go. God gives you His strategy. Your reward is certain!

EXCUSES

The villages were empty due to lack of warriors. Warriors were sloppy…*no fight* left in them.[16] Families had to run for their lives and entire villages were empty because there were no warriors who would stand up and fight. Four robbers are specifically called out by name.[17]

---

[15] Judges 4:14, *The Message*

[16] Judges 5:6-8

[17] Judges 5:16-18

Distractions kill the fight in you. Indecision. Reuben's divisions couldn't make up their minds. They were discussing warfare around the campfires. Debates about the best models of ministry don't rescue anyone. Talk is easy. Second-guessing accomplishes nothing. We must steward the day God has given us. This is our moment.

Gilead played it safe across the Jordan. Warriors dressed up yet paralyzed by fear. Fearful of men. Controlled by the opinions of others. Afraid to fail. Where will the finances come from? What will people think of my ability as a husband and father? Battles raging within that keep you from the fight you were formed to win.

Millions chained in darkness crying out in desperation for a deliverer and you are afraid to die. Only those who have died to themselves can have the wood laid on their backs. Carry your cross. Follow the Lord. Jesus is sending you. Live! In Jesus' name, live! I command you to be free from the spirit of fear and to live!

In my twenties, I made a decision to be included with those brave souls that take the challenge and go bungee jumping. Living in Missouri at the time, I heard about a location in Branson that would make this dream come true. I jumped in my car and raced from

Jefferson City to Branson. Seeing a crane high in the air, I made my way directly to the jump of a lifetime.

After signing all the papers…that any living relatives left could not sue should I die…things like that…I boldly walked over to that crane. Two young guys hooked me up by my ankles and immediately took me up 175 feet over a cement lot. Nothing below except hard, cold cement!

They opened the gate and casually said they would count to three and then I would jump straight out—headfirst…ankles attached to the cord. Well, while they were counting I was looking at how far below the tops of the trees were. I also noticed a man way down there eating a sandwich and looking up at me. It made me mad that I was his entertainment!

Two thoughts crossed my mind. One, my mother did not give birth to me to jump at a height of 175 feet from my ankles! Second thought, however, was very rational and intense. I had already paid the money (a lot for me at the time) and I was not getting that money back. I also instinctively knew I didn't want to be pushed out.

Get it together. Do this! And straight out I jumped. Racing toward the ground was surreal. Once caught by the bungee cord, every chemical in my body was released and *that* was quite a ride! Bring me a lion—I will tear it apart with my bare hands. Let's take on the world! I am one out of millions who actually has the guts to do this!

On reflection, I was forever impacted by this thought: Most people live their lives with their toes over the edge. Someone is counting...one, two, three...but they never jump. They are always *going* to do something for Jesus *some day*. They are going to sacrificially give. They are going to make a great impact. They are going *all in* for God.

They never actually take the risk. They are controlled by fear. They are ruled by excuses. They are content to compare themselves with others and never live the calling of God. They *will not* write on my tombstone: Played It Safe. *Never!* Jesus is worth my all. Jesus paid the ultimate price. His arms were stretched wide and He was lifted high for me!

No weapon formed against me can prosper. I am a servant of the Lord. I have the heritage of the servants of the Lord. I am in the lineage of the great prophets and apostles who gave their all for Jesus. I am desperate for Jesus! I am determined to give Him all of my heart, all of my soul, all of my mind, and all of my strength. He is worthy of all!

Selfishness is the third insidious thief. Dan went off sailing. In time of war, this tribe of warriors makes the decision to party! Pleasure is the idol of multitudes while millions perish without Jesus. It's not the time for self-indulgence. We are called to sacrifice. Take off your sailing gear and get your warrior's uniform on. Lace up your boots and get in this fight. It's your time!

Many churches were once vibrant centers of evangelism, aggressive in outreach overseas and fervent in prayer. They began to feel sleepy. This desire to lie down became an obsession for comfort and ease. As she fell into a deep sleep, the captain of a satanic army strapped cords of apathy, strings of discouragement, and ropes of weariness around this giant.

I am desperate for Jesus! I am determined to give Him all of my heart, all of my soul, all of my mind, and all of my strength. He is worthy of all!

The giant was trapped…tangled in the bonds of self-congratulations and shackled by the status quo. It's time to wake up! It's our moment to fight. Sleeping giants will rise again!

This song exposes one last excuse. The tribe of Asher kept their distance on the seacoast. They rationalized that the battle was so distant, so far away that it had nothing to do with them. What difference does Iran make to my life? Does ISIS have any impact on my salary and my daily priorities? The Middle East is so far, so distant. Come on warrior! God has formed you for this fight!

These pathetic warriors are in stark contrast to the men of Zebulun who risked their lives and they defied death. God chose *new leaders* who then fought at the gates. Just as Jesus came to the town gate of Nain and destroyed death, God is sending us to the places of authority in our world—the city gates—and they are coming down, in Jesus' name!

You must know that *God will restore your fight right now!* After this monumental triumph, there is peace for forty years. Midian oppression then choked the people of God for seven years. Judges 6:34 records that this time the warriors of Asher are willing to fight. A *new generation* of leaders rises up willing to rush into the battle and overcome.

God laid His hand on you. *Now* it's time for you to lay your hands on others. He has heard your desperate cry. He spoke life and broke the power of death over your life. *Now* you go in His name and speak freedom to the captives. This is your moment. God has marked you!

Oswald J. Smith personally gave more to missions every year than the salary paid to him from the church he pastored. God supernaturally provided. This outstanding pastor declared that there had never been a year since he became the pastor of the People's Church in Toronto when they used anything near as much on themselves at home as they had sent overseas to reach people in every nation on earth. Every year for fifty years, they held a missions convention that grew to four weeks and five Sundays…two services each day. No excuses. Desperation! Expectation! Transformation!

We are going to experience supernatural break-through in my generation. I am desperate before God. I will not settle for anything less. I invite you to come alongside of me. Together, it's on in Jesus' name!

Job prayed and his friends were delivered and God poured supernatural blessing into his life.

Moses prayed and the chosen ones of God marched boldly out of the furnace of slavery into a land overflowing with abundance.

God laid His hand on you. He spoke life and broke the power of death over your life. Now you go in His name and speak freedom to the captives. This is your moment. God has marked you!

Samson prayed and a thousand Philistines were killed with a donkey's jawbone.

Hannah prayed and God birthed in her a miracle son that led an entire nation back to God.

David prayed and witnessed the obliteration of God's enemies and experienced forgiveness for his sin.

Elijah prayed and a dead man came back to life.

Elijah prayed after three long years of drought and the skies opened and rain poured down.

Hezekiah prayed and 185,000 valiant soldiers of the Assyrian army were killed in one night by one angel.

Ezra prayed and Judah experienced revival.

Nehemiah prayed and the city wall was rebuilt and the temple of God restored.

Daniel prayed and the dreams of the king became understandable and the glory of the Ancient of Days was revealed.

Ten days of prayer in an upper room released Pentecostal fullness.

Stephen prayed and Jesus stood up.

Paul and Silas prayed and their chains unlocked, the earth quaked, and prison doors became open doors.

Martin Luther prayed and Europe bowed its knees and was transformed.

John Knox prayed, "Give me Scotland or I die!" Intensity births new realities.

Every morning when the sun came up, Hudson Taylor was on his knees praying and a new era in China's history commenced.

William Carey prayed and India received the Word of God in more than thirty different dialects.

David Livingstone opened up Africa and died on his knees praying for those close to the heart of God on that vital continent.

Wednesday, August 13, 1737 a gathering of fugitives in Moravia was praying when suddenly at 11:00 a.m. the Holy Spirit came and that prayer meeting continued for over one hundred years.

As Jesus was praying, the Holy Spirit descended on Him when He came up out of the water.

After praying all night, Jesus called twelve apostles to Himself and then sent them out in power and authority.

As Jesus was laying down His life on Calvary, He was praying for his ruthless persecutors.

Jesus is the resurrected Royal Son! He has **all** authority. He says to you, "Get up! It's your time!"

Judson endured unspeakable anguish in a Burmese prison. Thousands are tortured in labor camps across mainland China and in prison cells across Asia and the Middle East. Paul urged the Christ followers in Rome, "Understand the present time! Wake up! Put aside all deeds of darkness. Clothe yourself with the Lord Jesus Christ."[18]

Paul was not thrown off course by sleepless nights, rejection, humiliation, beatings, threats, violent storms, or the hostility of angry mobs ready to riot. Our eyes must be fixed on the Lamb who is worthy of our all. Clothe yourself with Jesus. Get up! He is the one who marked you with His resurrection life!

---

[18] Rom. 13:11-14

3

Encounter

He is altogether lovely.
—Song of Songs 5:16

The explosive power demonstrated on resurrection morning was ignited in Eden. When the sunrise of resurrection Sunday was more than four millennia in the distance, Almighty God drew a line in the sand before the belly of the serpent.

God not only knows the future—*He is* the beginning and He is the end. God made it clear that the serpent would bruise the Promised Seed on the heel. Jesus would decisively crush his head. The enemy's demise would come through the seed of a young teenager named Mary—chosen and highly favored by God.

The Savior was the Creator's only Son. Sin brought certain death. *Resurrection* would forever assassinate death!

Brutalized on Friday, Jesus was beautiful on Sunday. Tortured on Friday, Jesus was triumphant on Sunday. The sepulcher near Calvary was vacated after a mere thirty-six hours. Bloodshed. Battle. Brokenness. The rest of the story is this: Jesus is alive forevermore!

Hope arrived riding on a virgin donkey on the road between Jericho and Jerusalem commencing seven days that would revolutionize our world.

The pierced palms of the resurrected Lord soon overshadowed palm branches.

Monday – The tables of those who polluted His Father's house were overthrown.

Tuesday – Lunch at the home of Simon is interrupted by a woman's passion for Jesus. Expensive perfume covers Him and the fragrance lingers on His clothes as He carried His cross.

Wednesday – No one but Jesus knows His actions on this day. Silence. The Son of God attentive, riveted to the pulsating beat of His Father's heart.

Thursday – Judas. Greed. The feet bathed by the Lord Himself running into the night as the betrayer *sells his soul* for silver.

Friday – Cries of Gethsemane lead to crucifixion on Golgotha. The Eternal One paid the price for your emancipation. He died *as* you. Drops of His blood break your every chain.

Saturday – Jesus descends into the court of the king of terrors. He declares victory over every force of darkness. Jesus takes *all* authority and dominion back.

Sunday morning – Shaking. Spices. Sudden appearance of angels.

Last at the cross, first at the sepulcher, Mary Magdalene is the first to encounter her resurrected Lord. The curse of Eden is canceled by the conquest of Calvary. Jesus had cast seven demons out of Mary. She followed Him. She loves Him intensely. Tears streaming down her cheeks, Mary turns and sees Jesus standing there but thinks He is the gardener. Jesus calls her name. Encounter! Her life will never be the same again.

Jesus always keeps His word. God always gets the *last word*. The Promised Seed will rise again. *Christ is Lord!* He is the Royal Son forever!

Jesus commissions Mary to go to His brothers. The stone that locked the outside of the tomb is removed. The disciples are behind doors locked from the inside. Mary, breathless, races in with the message that transforms lives eternally: "I have seen the Lord!"[19]

---

[19] John 20:18

You must have a personal encounter with Jesus. You have been searching your whole life for your Father. You have been searching for love that lasts... for someone that will love you with his or her full attention and will not betray you, that will be intensely and forever devoted to you. When you encounter Jesus you encounter your *Father!*

You must have a personal encounter with Jesus. You have been searching your whole life for your Father. When you encounter Jesus you encounter your Father!

You cannot outrun the love of God. You are trying to numb that pain deep inside of you. You can't silence the voices within by earning millions of dollars. Multiple degrees from the best universities in the world will not quiet the insecurity and lack of confidence. Working endless hours in church to earn the approval of God doesn't cut it either.

Religion wants to punish. Religion screams, *It's never enough!* The scandal of grace is that God pursues you. God sets the table for you. God invites you. Jesus paid your penalty. His love never fails! Encounter the heart of God in this moment right now. God marks you...you are marked for encounter!

IMMERSED IN FIRE

Adam walked in the garden of God. Daily he experienced the fragrance of multiplied thousands of unique flowers, the beauty of sparkling gems, and the majestic colors of birds in flight. He drank from the cool waters of the river that flowed in the paradise of God.

Adam chose to go his own way. He turned his back on the God who had breathed life into him. God came to Adam. God called to Adam. God clothed Adam. Adam and his bride were driven out of the perfection of Eden as a consequence of their revolt. God placed on the east side cherubim and a *flaming sword* flashing back and forth.

God revealed Himself to Abram. God instructed him to take a heifer, goat, ram, dove, and a young pigeon. He cut them in half. The sun was setting. Thick, dreadful darkness came over Abram. God begins to speak to him about his destiny. Four hundred years of slavery would be followed by miraculous deliverance. God's chosen ones would come out with *great* possessions. In the darkness, Abram sees a smoking firepot with a *blazing torch*. Fire passes between the pieces of the sacrifice as God cuts covenant with a man.

Moses heard about the flaming sword at the entrance to the garden. He knew about the blazing torch that Abram saw. These encounters were real. Moses, banished from the palace of Egypt, leads the flock of his father-in-law to the far side of the desert. He comes to Horeb, the mountain of God.

The angel of the Lord appears to him in *flames of fire* from within a bush. Moses turns aside to look. Only after this decision, Moses hears the voice of God from within the fire. He receives a mandate to speak freedom to a nation.

God is drawing you close right now. Forty years is a long time to wait for an encounter with God. We just can't rush past this sacred moment. Take your shoes off. This is holy ground.

Art Katz writes in *Apostolic Foundations* as a man who has encountered the living God. He speaks of Moses' self-initiated conduct and this apostolic encounter. Moses looks this way and that and kills one Egyptian who is oppressing an Israeli slave. Moses buries one man in the sand. God intends to kill their entire army and bury them in the sea. Moses' posture is horizontal. He does not even consider looking up. Moses fails. Failure is God's way of setting you up for encounter![20]

Failure is God's way of setting you up for encounter!

Humiliation will rip self-sufficiency from your core. We will never be sent motivated by the needs in

---

[20] Art Katz, *Apostolic Foundations* (Bemidji, MN: Burning Bush Press, 2009), 12-22.

front of us. Moses is sent when He understands that *God heard* the cry of His people. God prepares you, marks you for this strategic mission.

You don't meet God in the spectacular. You encounter Him in dryness, disappointment, crushing pain, and in the inferior places.

When Moses encounters God, he is broken, empty, and disqualified in the natural to serve the living God. Trials, suffering, and failure birth in us the true knowledge of God. We are called to experience Him and to be His expression. We represent Him. Only the man who has encountered God can represent Him.

The rejected prince of Egypt has labored for forty monotonous, predictable years tending flocks. Absolutely nothing was lower in Egyptian values than this task. We will never lead a nation into deliverance until we labor in the ordinary and undistinguished.

Moses meets God in the backside of the desert. Horeb means dry, barren. You don't meet God in the spectacular. You encounter Him in dryness, disappointment, crushing pain, and in the inferior places.

YOUR CALL IS AN ETERNAL CALL

Your assignment and mandate on this earth are only a fraction of the fulfillment of the unique purpose for which God has called you. You understand this, right? You are marked by design for an *eternal call*. Oh how this transforms our perspective of absolutely everything! This reality must not only inform your mind. It must truly transform your very being! What is forty years of preparation in the light of fulfilling your unique purpose and design for eternal ages? The Sovereign Lord has marked you for eternity!

Are you willing to risk the loss of all things? There is no encounter, no calling, no holy ground, no sending, no national deliverance without laying it all down. Encounter is being immersed in the knowledge of God as He truly is that continually forms **you** into the message that makes God known to every living person.

The people of God, liberated from slavery, stand at the foot of Mount Sinai. God descended in fire and the whole mountain trembles violently. God instructs His people to daily offer whole burnt offerings. The fire must be kept burning on the altar throughout the entire night.

In God's dwelling place, the tabernacle, the golden lampstand with clear oil of pressed olives burns brightly. On the incense altar, the aroma of fragrant incense burns continually before the Lord. Every evening, the glory of God was over His dwelling place as a pillar of fire. When the millions of Israelis saw the fire, they knew God was present with them.

Elijah lived a life of fire. He confronted every idol and demonic stronghold on Carmel. The fire of the Lord fell and burned up the sacrifice, the wood, the stones, and the soil, and also licked up the water in the trench. God's chosen ones fell on their faces when the fire of God fell.

Elisha witnessed the chariot and horses of fire that suddenly appeared at Elijah's departure into the presence of God. When enemies surround Elisha, he exudes total confidence, aware that the hills were full of horses and chariots of fire all around him. God is present! Those supernaturally for us outnumber those who are against us. We need to see as God sees.

Those supernaturally for us outnumber those who are against us. We need to see as God sees.

Isaiah saw the Lord seated on His throne. Seraphs were calling to one another…Holy, Holy, Holy is the Lord Almighty. The very threshold of the temple shook. One of the seraphs flew to Isaiah with a live coal in his hand and touched his mouth. Oh, God, let my mouth be touched right now by Your fire!

Ezekiel saw a throne of sapphire. He saw one who from his waist up looked like glowing metal, full of fire. This majestic one from the waist down looked like fire. He was surrounded by brilliant light.

Daniel looked as the Ancient of Days took His seat. His throne was flaming with fire. A river of fire was flowing out from the presence of the Almighty One. Thousands upon thousands attended to Him and ten thousand times ten thousand stood before Him.

The fire of God, the river of God, is inside of you! His presence saturates you! You receive His power and you become His message. You are the fire of God every place you go.

Each of these encounters is saturated with revelation. Malachi declares that God will send His messenger to prepare the way before Him. He will come suddenly and He will come as a refiner's fire. He will purify!

For four hundred years, silence. No prophets. No word from the Lord. Then, John the Baptizer bursts into history declaring that One more powerful is coming who will immerse you in the Holy Spirit and in *fire!* What is John saying?

The same God who placed the flaming sword in Eden, the same blazing torch that Abram saw, the angel of the Lord who appeared in flames of fire within a bush, the chariots and horses of fire, the live coal of fire, the river of flowing fire, the refiner's fire—this same God is revealing Himself in Jesus! Jesus is here!

He will immerse you in His Spirit. He will immerse you in fire! The living God has revealed Himself to you. You can encounter Him right now.

How will I know this power is dwelling in me? Tongues of fire separated in the upper room and came to rest on 120 believers who were expecting the promise and gift of the Father. All of them were *filled* with the Holy Ghost.

The fire of God, the river of God, is *inside* of you! His presence saturates you! You receive His power and you become His message. You are the fire of God every place you go. Paul boldly told the followers of Christ: *Do not put out the Spirit's fire!* You are going to run with fire! You are going to declare Jesus to all nations. The fire of God is *in* you!

THE FIRE OF FRESH ENCOUNTER

The purpose of your encounter with Jesus is to release God's reign so His name is glorified forever. John said: "I looked and before me was a great multitude that no one could count from every nation, tribe, people and language standing before the throne and in front of the Lamb."[21] "These have been redeemed [purchased] from men as first fruits for God and the

---

[21] Rev. 7:9

77

Lamb."[22] All of history is moving toward the worship of the Lamb of God by every people group forever!

John Valentine Haidt painted the *First Fruits* exactly fifteen years from the date of the sending of the first Moravian missionaries. Jesus is painted in the center with people surrounding Him in distinctive dress. Each face painted portrayed a specific person—the first person who came to Christ from each nation where the Moravians were ministering. Those standing before the Lamb in that painting are from New England, St. John, the island of St. Thomas, Greenland, and many additional nations.

Vision is conceived in the heart of God. It is believed in the heart of His servant. It is achieved through partnership with the Holy Spirit. No daily encounter, no fire. Busyness without encounter is futile, useless movement. If you are not praying, you are just playing!

The sacred fire was never permitted to go out on the altar.[23] The fire of the Holy Spirit burning in Herrnhut led to fresh encounters every day. On August 13, 1727 the Holy Spirit was outpoured during a powerful Sunday communion celebration. Zinzendorf, their leader, was twenty-seven years old. As a direct result of the fire of God filling them, twenty-four men

[22] Rev. 14:4
[23] Lev. 6:13

and twenty-four women decided to invest one hour each day in scheduled prayer. That movement of fire continued for over one hundred years!

The fire resulted in Leonard Dober and David Nitschmann being sent out by the Herrnhut community as the first Moravian missionaries. From 1732-1742 this community of six hundred sent out more than seventy as full-time missionaries. Within twenty-eight years of Zinzendorf's leadership, this powerful church had sent out 226 missionaries!

The purpose of encounter is to experience Jesus and to be the burning expression of Jesus.

The purpose of encounter is to experience Jesus and to be the burning expression of Jesus. It is truly your life in the secret place of encounter that determines your eternal impact.

ONE ENCOUNTER CHANGES EVERYTHING

God desires to meet with you personally every day. The Bread of the Presence placed on the table in the tent of worship in the wilderness had to be *fresh*. Jesus taught us to pray: "Give us this day our daily bread."[24]

---

[24] Luke 11:3

Jesus is the *Bread of Life!* [25] It is my greatest desire to see Him every day, to hear His voice every moment, and to abide in His love with my every breath.

Encountering the presence of the living God will usher in reverence and awe.

Joshua encounters the Commander of the Army of the Lord with drawn sword in His hand. Joshua is commanded to *conquer* Jericho.[26]

Those who stay long in the secret place with Jesus act just like Him.

Manoah and his wife encounter the Angel of the Lord whose name is beyond understanding. They are commissioned to *raise* a son to lead a nation.[27]

Ezekiel encounters the Glorified One sitting on His throne. He is commanded to eat the scroll and sent to *prophesy* to the nation.[28]

John encounters the resurrected and glorified Jesus and falls at His feet as a dead man. He is charged to *write* what he has seen.

When God speaks with you, He will reveal Himself and what action is required of you. Those who stay long in the secret place with Jesus act just

---

[25] John 6:35
[26] Josh. 5:13-6:2
[27] Judges 13:17-21
[28] Ezek. 1:26-28

like Him. To express Jesus you must have a fresh encounter with Him.

Impossible bows down on the outside when Jesus rules your affections on the inside. You live by faith and total confidence in Him when He truly rules on the throne of your heart. Jesus is the most attractive person alive today. No one else comes close. You are reading these words because

> **Impossible bows down on the outside when Jesus rules your affections on the inside.**

He desires to mark your life every day as you encounter Him. When He walks into your room, you are in the presence of the only one who can fill the deepest desires of your heart.

You are perfectly loved. You are God's beloved. He is the Father you have been searching for your entire life. Do you have someone you can trust with the broken pieces of your heart? When we admit that we have chosen our own way and rejected God's perfect way we have started on that road to a new beginning. To follow Jesus, you have to deny yourself. Christ's unconditional love is drawing you close to God. It's your choice. It's your destiny.

Open your heart to Jesus with authentic words: "God, I believe You demonstrated Your love for me when Jesus died as me to receive the punishment for my sins. I open my heart to receive Your mercy. Your resurrection life is mine today and I begin anew with Jesus in control of my life.

When He walks into your room, you are in the presence of the only one who can fill the deepest desires of your heart.

Make me clean. Fill me with Your Holy Spirit right now. I will follow You." This is your moment for encounter!

When you encounter Jesus within the veil, you will never be the same again. My desire is to be a man who sits at the feet of Jesus within the veil. A. W. Tozer said: "Remember this: the man who has the most of God is the man that is seeking the most ardently for more of God."[29] He will increase your capacity and lavish you with Himself. Your hunger for Him will be filled!

WRESTLING WITH GOD

My life was greatly impacted by a message preached by Michael Dow. The revelation God gave him from Genesis 32 will rock you as well. Jacob encounters God for real!

"That night Jacob got up and took his two wives, his two maidservants, and his eleven sons and crossed the

---

[29] A. W. Tozer, *The Pursuit of God: The Human Thirst for the Divine* (Camp Hill, PA: WingSpread Publishers, 1982).

ford of the Jabbok. After he had sent them across the stream, he sent over all his possessions. So Jacob was left alone, and a man wrestled with him till daybreak. When the man saw that he could not overpower him, he touched the socket of Jacob's hip so that his hip was wrenched as he wrestled with the man. Then the man said, 'Let me go, for it is daybreak.' But Jacob replied, 'I will not let you go unless you bless me.'

The man asked him, 'What is you name?' 'Jacob,' he answered. Then the man said, 'Your name will no longer be Jacob, but Israel, because you have struggled with God and with men and have overcome.' Jacob said, 'Please tell me your name.' But he replied, 'Why do you ask my name?' Then he blessed him there. So Jacob called the place Peniel, saying, 'It is because I saw God face to face, and yet my life was spared.'"[30]

My desire is to be a man who sits at the feet of Jesus within the veil.

All of his life, Jacob tried to work his way into favor and blessing. He took the birthright from his brother Esau by manipulating his appetite. Esau's natural hunger for the stew Jacob prepared seemed of greater value than the birthright of his father. Jacob disguised himself to deceive his father and capture his

---

[30] Gen. 32:22-30

blessing. Striving. Working. Deceiving. Now Jacob finds himself *alone*. He is about to face Esau again after years on the run.

The last words out of his brother's mouth vowed to murder Jacob. Jacob's heart is tormented with the burden of how is he going to fix this mess he's in. Oh, how many hours I have spent in this prison. How can I do something to fix the mess I am in? *Doing. Doing. Doing.*

Jesus did it all for us. Until we encounter Him in power, we will never be liberated from that prison cell of self-sufficiency.

Jesus did it all for us. Until we encounter Him in power, we will never be liberated from that prison cell of self-sufficiency. Be free, in Jesus' name! Just lay it all down before Him. You don't have the strength to fix it anyway. Only God can transform a person's heart and give you favor. Only His verdict on your life really matters anyway.

All night. How serious are you to encounter God Himself? God wants your absolute attention. What are you expecting when you say you want Him? This will not be some fifteen-minute devotional in the car on the way to work. He is going to wrestle with you until transformation takes place. One on one. God and you. Close. Face to face. Nothing hidden from Him.

God asks Jacob: "What is your name?" There it is! God *knows* the answer to that question. Why is He asking him then? He is forcing Jacob to confront the issues, the deception, the dark *inside* of him. God is calling out the you inside of you!

Your name is deceiver. God is calling out the Israel that He has formed in you! Don't limit God. Don't place labels on people: dreamer; prodigal; immoral; useless. God sees the great man of God in you that will proclaim His message

God is calling out the you inside of you!

and most importantly live close to His heart all of your days. God touches the socket of Jacob's hip. What do people see by your walk? It's not your talk that matters. When the fire of God burns in you, your walk is transformed!

ENCOUNTERING LOVE

Very early in the morning I made my way in the crisp New England air to a gathering of young adults. That's when I saw her. Beautiful, long-flowing hair. White blouse perfectly buttoned. Dark skirt. High heels. She was walking back and forth praying.

Clearly, she was intense and disciplined. She had an intentional pursuit of God. I made meeting that princess my priority. I'm married to RainyDawn today and she is the delight and joy of my life. Our partnership, union, and intense love are the reason I am who I am today.

Understand that *today* is God's gift to you. You must maximize every breath to please the one who gave *His* best for you. Embrace these realities:

Jesus is your identity. Ministry is not what defines you. Strength comes as you allow the Holy Spirit, moment by moment, to make real to you Christ's unconditional love *for you!* Experience His mercy daily. Make Christ the *center* of your relationships and decisions. This births freedom to say no to the unrealistic expectations of others. Fear of failure is transformed into the excitement of knowing Christ is pleased with you.

God chose you to change the world. Life is not a game. Millions with no access to a Christ follower or the Gospel of the Kingdom are only going to have an opportunity to choose eternal life as we obey His mandate to go to them. Planting churches in zero-access zones is priority in my life, our family, and the church in New York City that my wife and I serve as pastors. We give sacrificially because we value every unreached person and we are passionate about the name of Jesus being known to every person breathing.

It's all about love. Reverse evangelism was going on in a once-strong church. These believers had started well. Now they were arguing, bragging, exploiting the poor, and full of themselves. The spirit of Corinth had permeated these believers. Paul made it clear that without love nothing else matters. He uses verb after verb to describe real love in action. Love has a long fuse. Love is useful. Love celebrates the excellence of others. Love never shows off. Love is not rude. Love gives of yourself to strengthen others. It's not irritable.

True love keeps no record of wrongs. Love does not delight in what breaks God's heart but rejoices when truth prevails. Love carries possibilities. Love always trusts. Love knows that with God all things are possible. Love never looks back but keeps going strong to the end.

God's supernatural love is in you. You are marked by encounter. Experience the passion of His burning heart today!

4

Covenant

Jonathan made a covenant with David because
he loved him as himself.
—1 Samuel 18:3

God desires to be close to you. Your Father in
heaven who possesses unlimited power and all
authority yearns moment by moment to know you.
This intense longing is not birthed out of obligation.
His heart to lavish His love on you and be your closest
friend is motivated by unconditional, perfect, and
never-ending love. His thoughts are always on you.

I want you to truly comprehend this reality. There
is never a nanosecond that the living, all-powerful God
is not thinking about you. Daily He is composing and
singing original love songs over your life. The intensity

of the relationship He is inviting you into is revealed in covenant.

Our generation knows by experience the sting of multiplied broken relationships. Trust shattered. Hearts pierced. As we are created in the image of God, we carry this longing for unbroken relationship. You have a Father. He eternally exists in union with the Son and Spirit.

He is calling you into their perfect union. He *designed you* to be *with Him* forever. Jesus is the portal into the covenant of redemption that can never be destroyed.

Jesus is the portal into the covenant of redemption that can never be destroyed.

Jesus is absolutely trustworthy. He lived the perfect life we could not live. He died *as* us taking our torture and punishment for sin. He was raised from death so we can supernaturally be born from above. He is now seated in authority with His Father. Jesus is everything!

Jesus is the gateway. Entering in His life, we let go of all the failure of our past and are filled with the inexpressible joy of knowing Him, loving Him, and hosting His presence. His face now captivates our every breath!

Abram, the man God delighted in as a close friend, encounters the God who desires to cut covenant with us. The living God is speaking directly to you right now, as you become an eyewitness to God's encounter with Abram.

SET UP BY GOD

"After this, the word of the Lord came to Abram in a vision."[31] After what? What set up an ordinary, finite mortal for the eternal God coming to him? This encounter takes place directly after a fierce battle. Lot, Abram's nephew, carried an intense father wound. Haran, the father of Lot, died in the land of his birth. Lot grew older; however, his heart did not mature as he found it difficult to connect with the God of promise.

Entering in His life, we let go of all the failure of our past and are filled with the inexpressible joy of knowing Him, loving Him, and hosting His presence.

Lot has the unique honor of traveling with Abram. He personally heard his uncle speak about God's promise to bless Abram and make him a great nation. He had access to the revelation that all peoples on earth would be blessed through one coming from this family. Abram walked closely with God. He built altars to the Lord. Lot was physically close to a man that desired to know God. He had multiple opportunities

[31] Gen. 15:1

to worship with Abram. Yet it is clear that Lot's heart is self-absorbed.

When Abram takes action to resolve conflict between those working for Lot and those working for Abram, Lot "chose for himself" the whole plain of the Jordan and settled near Sodom.[32] Abram yields to God's design and promise spoken over his life. He walks in obedience to His promise. He is surrendered to God and will not live to manipulate God.

BEING HELD HOSTAGE

Lot's downward spiral into destruction accelerates until he is living in the center of evil and is taken captive by enemy armies. He doesn't embrace the Father heart of God and carries no authority in his life. His family is taken captive because he is captive in his own heart. He needs a deliverer. He has lost everything. Freedom is gone. Hope has died. His family is being held hostage. All the goods and all the food of Sodom are now controlled by enemy powers.

God intervenes and rescues in His mercy. Abram is informed that his relative is now a prisoner of war. Abram will not accept this outcome as permanent. His understanding of the heart of God and the promises covering his family move him into immediate action.

---

[32] Gen. 13:11

Passive people do not inherit the kingdom of God. When you know God's heart toward you and you live in covenant closeness with your Father, you will never tolerate the work of the enemy in your life. You will stand up for your family, your city, and your world. It's time to call out the trained men. It's time to push into the fight. We have the authority of Jesus within us!

"When Abram heard that his relative had been taken captive he called out his 318 trained men born in his household and went in pursuit as far as Dan."[33] When we live in covenant we train those born in our household. We have men alert, armed, and positioned to fight immediately when called. We are willing to pursue...to go after *all* that God has for us. We go as far as it takes until we have the full measure that God designed for us.

> **When you know God's heart toward you and you live in covenant closeness with your Father, you will never tolerate the work of the enemy in your life.**

God fills Abram with His strategy. During the night, he divides his men and attacks. He recovers *everything*. Where does this strength that endures through the night come from? Where does superior

---

[33] Gen. 14:14

strategy and perfect wisdom originate? How do you ever press forward, alert and active to pursue all God has for you? It comes from a sustained gaze.

It is only the reality of those whose lives are given to knowing God Himself. It is birthed in relationship with Him. This life continually intensifies as you are immersed in God Himself. Nothing of eternal value exists separate from the life of God within us. Abram carries the promise of God inside of him at all times. We carry the presence of Jesus inside of us at all times.

BREAD AND WINE

Battles come and our triumph is assured when the life of God dwells within us. What action does this man of faith take in this exhilarating moment when all that was stolen is recovered? How does he move forward once he experiences this grace to overcome and possess all?

"Then Melchizedek king of Salem brought out bread and wine. He was priest of God Most High, and he blessed Abram saying, 'Blessed be Abram by God Most High, Creator of heaven and earth. And blessed be God Most High, who delivered your enemies into your hand.' Then Abram gave him a tenth of everything."[34] He responds with humility and generosity.

---

[34] Gen. 14:18-20

Abram recognizes that *God* delivered him. He understood that every perfect gift came from God Most High. He knew it was God's strength *in him* that destroyed enemies. He knew his possessions were not his own. He willingly returns a tenth. Most important, bread and wine are brought out to him. This was the action of a priest and speaks of encounter and authentic relationship.

It is only in covenant relationship with God, through Jesus, that we can know God personally.

This is God's desire to commune with us. God comes to us and invites us to be one with Him. It is only in covenant relationship with God, through Jesus, that we can know God personally. God desires for us to eat with Him, to be in continual communion with Him, and to be saturated and lavishly immersed in Him.

God is setting Abram up for a life-changing vision. How does God prepare the man and woman that He has marked by design? Enemies roar and God personally leads us to deliverance. He comes to us now *as the* bread and wine inviting us into Himself. We desire Him above all others. We embrace His pursuit of us and run into His strong arms. We return the tenth. We give our everything to Him!

VOWS

Abram is met by another king right before God comes in the vision. The king of Sodom comes and offers Abram all the goods recaptured in the war. This Gentile king wants to give Abram all the material possessions rightfully belonging to the victor.

Although Abram allows those men fighting with him to have their share, he will not allow anyone other than God Himself to be his source. "I have raised my hand to the Lord God Most High… and have taken an oath that I will accept nothing belonging to you…so that you will never be able to say 'I made Abram rich.'"[35]

The setup for the vision is God breaking the heart of the man He has destined to use to reveal Himself to all generations. Abram personally experiences the strong power of God over vicious enemies. He over-flows with humility when God comes to him in the bread and wine. He willingly gives and refuses to take for himself. He has set his heart on God alone.

His gaze is fixed. No looking back. No longing for what once was. He is a man who burns with the words of God within him. He overcomes in the intense conflict over his enemies on the outside and wins the battle for the affection of his heart within.

---

[35] Gen. 14:22-23

He knows how to walk as a victor without being arrogant. He trusts God completely and God alone as his source!

TRUE REWARD

After this, Abram sees the Word. God pursues him. God comes to him and nothing will ever be the same after this encounter. The greatest vision God will ever give a mortal is of Himself...as your exceedingly great reward. He is the only true and eternally satisfying reward.

God's first word to the man He desires to use emphatically declares that fear cannot stand.

The greatest vision God will ever give a mortal is of Himself... as your exceedingly great reward.

"Do not be afraid, Abram. I am your shield."[36] When God Himself has captivated our vision, His perfect love obliterates fear.

Abram's descendants hundreds of years later would be snatched out of the brutal slavery of Egypt and marched boldly armed for battle through the towering walls of water of the Red Sea. When they saw their enemies dead on the shore, they burst into exuberant singing with these powerful lyrics:

---

[36] Gen. 15:1

"Who among the gods is like you, O Lord?
Who is like you—majestic in holiness,
    awesome in glory, working wonders?
You stretched out your right hand and the
    earth swallowed them.
In your unfailing love you will lead the people
    you have redeemed.
In your strength you will guide them to your
    holy dwelling.
The nations will hear and tremble; anguish
    will grip the people…
The chiefs of Edom will be terrified; the
    leaders of Moab will be seized
with trembling, the people of Canaan will melt
    away; terror and dread will
fall upon them."[37]

Their hearts gaze on the majesty, holiness, unfailing love, strength, and purpose of the living God working in them. There is zero fear, and with confidence they know God will fulfill His promise and bring them into an inheritance of abundance. How then do they later reject God's purpose and collapse in fear, speaking death to each other?

---

[37] Ex. 15:11-16

Instead of their enemies trembling, the people of God are shaking and have convinced themselves in toxic unbelief that they are like grasshoppers in the eyes of these giants. Fear enters when we take our gaze off of our true reward—God Himself!

Fear enters when we take our gaze off of our true reward— God Himself! No fear exists in my life when I understand by experience that God is my shield.

No fear exists in my life when I understand by experience that God is my shield. He is my continual strength. He is the warrior that goes in front of me. His power infuses every facet of my being. One breath from God's mouth and every adversary of mine perishes. What confidence we live in today when we make the choice to be still and know Him!

"I am your exceedingly great reward."[38] So many are driven by the pursuit of rewards that quickly evaporate. Their hearts are lured and enticed by temporal symbols that vanish without warning. When God reveals Himself to us personally as our *exceedingly* great reward, there are no lovers that can compare with His perfection. The Sovereign over all is the very one who marked your life by design!

---

[38] Gen. 15:1

TOXIC VOICES

The immediate verbal response of Abram to this revelation is shocking. "O Sovereign Lord, what can you give me since I remain childless and the one who will inherit my estate is Eliezer of Damascus? ... You have given me no children; so a servant in my household will be my heir."[39] Hold on! Abram addresses Him as *sovereign* and then is fixated on his own lack. What?

The living God reveals that He is your greatest reward and Abram cannot see how that relates in any way to Almighty God fulfilling what He had already vowed to Abram. It was already revealed to him that all nations of the earth would be blessed through his literal descendants. Open your heart to see the connection. God Himself fulfills every word He speaks.

It is sadly very possible to sing to God, read the Word of God, be surrounded by people who claim to follow God, and yet in your own soul be focused on your lack. God, I just don't see how You are fulfilling Your promise to me. How much longer, Father? My present situation sure doesn't line up with the vision You gave me for my life. If I am truly marked by design, then where is the evidence that You are with me?

---

[39] Gen. 15:2-3

Listen! God Himself is your reward. When you are merged with Him and He has pulled you into *His life*, you must allow *His presence* in you to silence the toxic voices fighting to keep you choked with fear. Do not feed the fiery shrill of unbelief that pierces like an arrow into your spirit. The fire of God is stronger. The voice of God is stronger. The vision of God is stronger. The covenant God has established with you will never fail and can never be destroyed!

When you are merged with Him and He has pulled you into His life, you must allow His presence in you to silence the toxic voices fighting to keep you choked with fear.

Fix your eyes on Jesus. You can't make it happen. Exactly! The longer you are driven by your futile attempts to bring the future vision into today, you will fail to see the vision of this moment. God Himself is that vision!

RAISE THE ROOF

I love what God does next. He directly confronts unbelief. If you choose to play with the viper of doubt you will die. God is clear that the heir of promise will come directly from Abram's own body. Supernatural. All God! Then he "took him outside."[40] Don't miss

---

[40] Gen. 15:5

this strategic word. It doesn't say Abram decides to go outside. It doesn't even say God told him to go outside. There is undeniable intentionality in this word...God *took* him outside. It's time to let God take you by your arm and lead you exactly where He wants to position you so you can hear from Him.

I love written plans. I typed fourteen pages of instructions in preparation for our wedding ceremony. We had eight pastors participating from seven different states. Chinese church leaders flew in from Asia and honored us. More than six hundred guests packed into the sanctuary in New York City to celebrate with us. We had written plans!

God desires to burst into our written plans and take us out of our limited comprehension to plunge us into the immensity of who *He* is and His extravagant design for us! God takes Abram out of his tent. Michael Dow, in his life-transforming book *The Breaking Point*,[41] speaks to this exact moment when God thrusts Abram into a fresh perspective.

"Look up at the heavens and count the stars—if indeed you can count them. So shall your offspring be."[42] In the inky blackness of that night, the Word of the Lord is visible. Abram is called to look up. He is eyewitness to the radiance of God's glory in those

---

[41] Michael Dow, *The Breaking Point*, (Burning Ones, 2015), 207-211.
[42] Gen. 15:5

millions of shining stars. Their brightness pierces the dark questions in Abram's inner man. The creative word that spoke these stars into existence is from the identical mouth of the One who is *now* speaking with Abram.

It's time to let God take you by your arm and lead you exactly where He wants to position you so you can hear from Him.

Why did God take him outside? Abram lived a life-long journey traveling and staying in tents. He was accustomed to this life. Permanence was foreign to his experience. I was raised in Brooklyn. However, I do know this about tents…the roof is *too* low. Dwelling in tents can lull you into believing that your current roof is as high as you will ever go.

Normal is small. Normal is limited. Normal is confined. God *took* him outside to see the heavens and to gaze far beyond the natural heavens and to breathe in the atmosphere of God's throne. God wants you today to not only look up and see the natural; He is calling you to look up all the way into His dwelling place…where His glory resides. Look at *Him*. Desire Him.

God commanded him to count the stars. What is it going to take before you realize just how limited your power is? We can't even count what God has already created. So why are you striving to create your future? God has arrested your attention, led you outside, and is now speaking His vision into your life. Let go! You can't count the stars no matter what strategy you devise. Let go! Let Him in! Listen to what He is speaking over you. Let Him free you from your low ceiling.

What is it going to take before you realize just how limited your power is? We can't even count what God has already created. So why are you striving to create your future?

Right now, encounter Him. You are not just reading a book. God Himself is ripping that roof off and intensely and lavishly pouring Himself into you. Welcome Him. Speak to Him. He will increase your capacity for His presence, you know. You will thirst to be with Him. You will be immersed in Him and you will still long for more of Him.

Like the wife you made your vows to and the closest brother that you love, you can never have enough time listening to their voice…being with them. Being in their presence creates the craving for more time to experience them. Like the young lovers who can't go their separate ways at the end of a perfect evening, you will long for Jesus.

You will no longer be limited by the narrow confines of your little tent. You can never be satisfied again living with people who can't see past their pathetic roofs. You will long for Jesus. You will never want to go back inside again!

You will walk in the darkest night under the brilliance of His glory and embrace Him who is life itself. God marked *you* for this. This living in covenant intimacy with your exceedingly great reward—God Himself—is why you exist!

This is the moment when Abram believes God and experiences His righteousness. This is the encounter that moves into God commanding Abram to bring to Him the specific animals with which God will cut covenant with His friend. God will come as a smoking firepot with a blazing torch and pass between the pieces of the sacrifice. Abram is placed in a deep sleep, for this covenant depends on God alone and not the best intentions or efforts of any mortal.

This living in covenant intimacy with your exceedingly great reward—God Himself—is why you exist!

Can you still hear His voice? Is the voice inside you louder than His covenant promise? Are the other voices inside the tent still calling to you? Come back inside, Abram, where it is safe! Haven't you stayed out there long enough, Abram? We're having a great time in here. You have to be practical, Abram. Looking up doesn't pay the bills. Stay balanced, bro. What are you doing for so long out there all alone? You are never alone! You are drinking in Jesus! You have the bread and wine of His presence!

Never settle down back inside that tent. Never allow the voices of carnality and low living to drown the voice of your great reward. Trust me. God has designed new voices for your life that will speak in agreement with His covenant love!

COVENANT BROTHERS

God's desire to reveal Himself to us is so intense that He will choose a brother and commission them into your life. Jesus is the perfection of God in His fullness. The perfect God-Man prayed all night and then called men to Himself.

This calling is much more than a mandate to do things in Jesus' name. Jesus desires close relationship. His heart is to do life with real brothers. We are marked for deeply authentic, genuine, heart connection with brothers who are all in with Jesus!

David, the warrior poet, penned this revelation: "The Lord confides in those who fear him. He makes his covenant known to them. My eyes are ever on the Lord."[43] He lived in that secret place where God delights to reveal His most intimate thoughts to a man.

David's first ministry was always to the Lord Himself personally. His every breath was yielded to gazing on the face of the Lord. David embraced the field. He loved the presence of God and breathed that rarefied air of continual worship and communion with God Himself.

David is uniquely known as the man after God's own heart. His understanding of God's heart was the overflow of doing life with a covenant brother that God supernaturally brought to him. After David is anointed to be the future king, He goes back to the fields. Sent by his father, only then does he go to the front lines of battle. The Israelis are running in fear from one man instead of demonstrating the power of their covenant God.

David hears the taunts of Goliath *once* and runs toward that fight in the strength of God. The trained warriors cowered in fear eighty consecutive times. They had no understanding of the heart of God. David declares exactly what God will do to this adversary and reveals His motive. God will give this enemy over to David so that the whole world will know there is

---

[43] Psalm 25:14-15

one true living God that has established His covenant with the people of Israel!

A GREATER GIFT

The triumph over evil is astounding, yet God has a greater gift for David than the head of this giant. God has purposed that the man He has anointed will experience the fullness of God's heart toward him. While the blood of Goliath is still dripping, God establishes residence in the heart of Prince Jonathan and marks him as a covenant brother for David.

The greatest life you can ever experience is being yielded to the adventure of Jesus' call to *come*, follow *Him!* He orders your steps. Jesus is in the front. He designs the relationships that will transform you into the man or the woman that He has designed.

Jonathan comes to David. He doesn't offer a contract. Jonathan makes a covenant with David. Spiritual, God breathed, sealed in the heart. This is a relationship birthed by the Holy Spirit and is unbreakable and enduring. Jonathan makes the choice to lose himself in someone else.

David's natural brothers despise him. His oldest brother accuses and slanders him. He mocks his assignment with those few sheep as insignificant. Jonathan has the heart of God toward David. He loves him as he loves himself. He willingly strips off his robe with the royal insignia and places it on David.

This prophetic demonstration is the revelation of God's heart toward His chosen servant and the pulse of God's heart toward you.

When you can't even believe in yourself, when every natural voice around you mocks the vision that is pulsating within you, God will send you a covenant brother that will breathe the life of God into you again. *You* can choose your friends. It is *God* that ordains covenant relationships. You will be sideswiped by the glory of God, and when you look up…there is Jesus standing before you clothed in a covenant brother!

When every natural voice around you mocks the vision that is pulsating within you, God will send you a covenant brother that will breathe the life of God into you again.

Here is how God set me up. On a Monday night in 2014, I decided to watch a television broadcast of Christ for All Nations. Reinhard Bonnke came to Shanghai in the beginning years of our ministry there. Having the opportunity to hear his heart in person and eat with him marked my life. This man yielded completely to Jesus has transformed millions.

This broadcast, however, was with several young leaders who were each speaking and interacting together. When the young man wearing a cool bright shirt and light-colored shoes, sitting at the end of the row directly in front of the camera spoke, there was an explosion of the Spirit inside of me. I will never have the eloquence to write what I experienced. It was a supernatural moment and revelation from God that I was going to be connected with him, strongly connected! I knew this man was totally different than most people I had met just listening to him speak. He knew Jesus, and that was intensely evident!

I discovered his name: Michael Dow. He had recently written his first book, *Free Indeed.* I sensed the next step was simply to order the book, read it, and find out what this man was all about. When that first book arrived in New York City at the Leadership Center of the church I serve as pastor, Michael had placed a second copy with it. He had written a short note saying he felt the Holy Spirit impressed on him to send the second one as a gift.

Seemingly insignificant steps of obedience lead to *significant* breakthroughs! When I read that note, the Holy Spirit forcefully spoke to me that this was a man of integrity, a man who followed the voice of the Lord, a man that I could trust.

In reading *Free Indeed,* my heart was broken by Jesus as He was preparing me for a unique encounter with Himself. Here was a young man that was writing insights that could only come from a very intimate walk with Jesus. His understanding of the heart of Jesus was astonishing to me. I felt directed to order additional books and began to give them as gifts to young ministers that were important in my life.

Months went by and on occasion we would exchange e-mails. I was waiting on God to arrange for us to meet in person in His timing. In the fall of 2014, I sent an e-mail saying that I would love to eat with him sometime whenever he was in the New York City area. Michael responded that he had a dream and that he and his wife Anna were going to fly to New York City, at their own expense, just to have a meal with my wife RainyDawn and me. I was impacted by his generosity and clearly knew that it was God's heart putting all of this together.

This takes us to the weekend of November 21-23, 2014. Nothing would be the same after this weekend. In my mind, I still thought Michael was coming to NYC to preach somewhere and the meal with us was just something he was adding to the ministry weekend. Eventually I asked him in a text where he was going to be on Sunday, November 23. I will never forget his answer. He simply wrote: "With you."

Here was a man and his wife who were greatly used of God willing to come to NYC at their own expense just to love a pastor and his wife that they had never met in person. We had never even spoken over the phone together. He was going to come on Sunday and just sit and listen to me minister the Word. Was this for real?

I immediately asked him to see if Jesus would release him to preach at 11 a.m. in the church we serve. Jesus said yes. Now, I am a pastor that has one or two guest speakers max on Sunday in an entire year. Here was a Jesus preacher I had never met coming to preach and I absolutely knew God was pleased and this was His design.

The Friday and Saturday with Michael and Anna was unlike any guests we had ever hosted before. They loved speaking about Jesus. They were intense, no excuses, all in, wildly in love with Jesus. They carried His presence and it was so refreshing!

The Friday they arrived we ate lunch together in Manhattan. Friday night my wife joined us and we sat down in a German restaurant for dinner. Michael and Anna pulled out two beautiful white boxes and presented them as gifts to us. I was shocked. Speechlessly shocked. When I opened the box for me, it was such an amazing watch and so unexpected I thought I was going to have to leave the table so they would not see me cry. Even then, I couldn't understand my own reaction. Jesus was at that table. He had brought a covenant brother to me. I was marked by design.

Sunday at 11 a.m. the church was packed. When we walked into that sanctuary together, the tangible presence of Jesus was there. I now understand that when a man seeks God literally for hours every day and his only desire is for Jesus to come into the room and to have His own way, the supernatural is natural! Oh how my heart bleeds for the thousands who go in and out of church buildings every week and never encounter Jesus Himself!

I now understand that when a man seeks God literally for hours every day and his only desire is for Jesus to come into the room and to have His own way, the supernatural is natural!

Our worship team honored Jesus and Michael came to the front. He described a woman he saw in prayer that would be in the service and would be healed by Jesus. She was there. She was healed even before the message started. The message was a true word in season from Matthew 16. All Jesus!

The invitation to follow Jesus was bold and direct. Decisions to deny yourself and follow Jesus were made. Miracles of healing took place. At 3:30 p.m. young adults were still at the altar seeking Jesus! After praying for so many people, I sat down on the steps right next to the pulpit.

When I looked up, I saw Michael laying hands on the people still coming to meet with Jesus. We had literally already prayed for hundreds of people. In that moment, the Spirit of God came into me in a fresh way and I knew it was what Jonathan felt for David after his bold demonstration of the power of God's name.

This was not just natural friendship. This was a covenant brother assigned to me to lead me to the burning heart of Jesus and stay with me there.

This was not just natural friendship. This was not just a guest speaker who really blessed the church. This was a covenant brother assigned to me to lead me to the burning heart of Jesus and stay with me there. This was the birthing of a new season. Before flying back to Orlando that same night, he explained that the timepiece was the sign of the prophetic word of the Lord to us: "Your time is now."

From that Sunday to this very day, God has fastened us into oneness. Michael told me, "Transparency with God produces vulnerability before men." A covenant brother can see the habitation of God in the man standing in front of him. Jesus places within you the willingness to literally lay down your life for that brother. There are no strings attached. It is a relationship based on what Jesus has done for us.

Eric Gilmour, in his God-inspired book *Burn*, nailed it when he said covenant brothers are *in* one another! These relationships are not marked by jealousy, competition, and the self-promotion so disgusting among too many ministers. Covenant brothers live to honor the brother that Jesus has given to them. When you honor that brother, you are honoring Jesus Himself.

David Popovici, a powerful lover of Jesus, lives covenant. Listen to his heart!

1. Covenant that is divine is initiated by and sealed by the Spirit. Jonathan and David would be an example. It cannot be legislated or coerced but should be developed once established.

2. A covenant man (David in Scripture which to me is one of the greatest examples) naturally draws to himself other people with like heart. With that said, it is very difficult if not altogether impossible to covenant with dozens of people. One can have strong relationships but not what I would define as a deep covenant relationship. Jesus only had twelve, and even within that sphere, the three and the one that He covenanted with. That is not coincidental.

3. Covenant relationships in the Kingdom are built upon first love for Father-Son-Spirit before anything, Jesus being the *ultimate* example of a covenant man. Not primarily personality type or gifting.

4. Covenant relationships should be more sacredly cherished, protected, and invested in than other relationships.

5. One should seek to, through prayer, natural means and the giving of oneself to seek to advance the presence, image, and call of God on his brother's life.

6. There should be a code of love, honor, respect, and the Christ-like humility that ever prefers and deems one's brother's welfare as more important than one's own.

7. Covenant is built upon friendship, vulnerable trust, and love unto death. Jesus said no longer do I call you just servants but "friends" because Jesus vulnerably gives Himself to us. The greatest kind of love is willing to give all.[44]

Jesus established the new covenant with us by laying down His life. We merge with Him under the waters

---

[44] E-mail from David Popovici about Covenant, 2014.

of baptism. His resurrection life in us now confronts the powers of darkness everywhere we place our feet. He commissions covenant brothers. Covenants are for life! Your life is marked by covenant.

5

Released

"I have but one passion—it is He, it is He
alone. The world is the field, and the field is
the world; and henceforth that country shall
be my home where I can be most used in
winning souls for Christ."
—Zinzendorf[45]

The arena is charged. You are standing in the place
where battles are fought. Conflict permeates the
air. Sounds of revolution shoot throughout the city.

One hundred thirty million youth...teenage
students with red arm bands on their left sleeve and

---

[45] Nikolaus Ludwig von Zinzendorf, "Missions and Evangelism
Quotes," *Tentmaker,* http://www.tentmaker.org/Quotes/evange-
lismquotes.htm.

holding little red books filled with quotations of Mao are screaming for justice. Justice! Radio stations across China are playing militant martial music. Thousands of voices shout in unison that the east wind is prevailing over the west wind. The communists rocked China. The east wind blew furiously.

I am not committed to a cause. I am committed to a person!

Jesus understood that the wind blows wherever it wants. He was not speaking of a wind from the east or from the west. He testified that He was an eyewitness to the wind from heaven above.

In a sparsely furnished room, in a home meeting, suddenly a sound from heaven roared. The rushing, mighty, violent wind from the throne filled that house. Fire filled those that were obedient to sit with Jesus in His presence and to *not do anything* until they were endued with *His* power.

Jesus told His closest followers that once He ascended to the Father, He would no longer be standing beside them on the outside. They were marked by design to do *greater things* than even Jesus did because now Jesus was going to *stand up inside* of them!

YOU CANNOT IMPRISON THE WIND

The communists arrogantly declared that they would kill the church. They boasted that they would end the apostolic movement bringing transformation to that nation. Their leaders bragged that they had the ability to stop this wind from heaven. The communists destroyed thousands of Bibles, arrested pastors, and brutally and publicly murdered the followers of Jesus.

No one can imprison the wind! One hundred million Chinese followers of Jesus today living in mainland China are evidence of the unstoppable resurrection life-giving power of God. We have a mandate from Christ Himself. I am not committed to a cause. I am committed to a person!

Jesus is the Lamb that was slain. He laid down His life. No one took it from Him. He *will* receive the reward of His sufferings. Your life laid down totally for Him is His reward. He pursued you. He longed for you. He formed you in the womb and then apprehended you to lavish His grace on you and to *empower* you to transform nations in His name!

Every moment of every day I am yielding to God. I continually and intentionally invite Jesus to baptize me in the Holy Spirit.

Being immersed in the fire of the Holy Ghost is not a one-time experience. Every moment of every day I am yielding to God. I continually and intentionally invite Jesus to baptize me in the Holy Spirit. The Holy Spirit reveals Jesus to me. He empowers me to burn everywhere so that those in the darkest and most distant places will be loosed and set free in the name of Jesus. The fire of the Holy Spirit will not be stopped. You can never lock up the wind of God.

HEARTBEAT OF GOD

Yield to the Spirit of God. Let Him take you again to Jesus. Lean back on His chest. The Holy Ghost will awaken your ears to hear the very heartbeat of God. Being led by the Spirit is walking in the rhythm of God set by the heartbeat of God.

God's desire has always been to reveal Himself to all nations!

Abraham interceded on behalf of the cities of Sodom and Gomorrah. Jacob stood before Pharaoh and blessed him.

Joseph triumphed over every adversity. Thousands of lives were saved and nations transformed through this man living in the favor of God.

As Moses was receiving the revelation written by the finger of God on two stone tablets, Hinduism was being birthed.

As Isaiah was prophesying for all nations to look to the covenant God, to turn to Him and be saved, Siddhartha was leaving the luxury of the palace and beginning to teach the precepts of Buddhism.

Ezekiel was a watchman who experienced the glory of God and spoke the decrees of God as Confucius had three thousand students in training when he was thirty-four years old.

Hananiah, Azariah, and Mishael stood boldly in the pagan throne room of Nebuchadnezzar. They defied the brash young dictator and became the revelation of the delivering power of their covenant God.

Jesus came weeping over the city. He is the radiance of the Father's glory. To see Jesus is to encounter all the fullness of God. He is the exact representation of the heartbeat of God. He was filled with compassion for people who did not seize their moment when God personally came to them.

Being led by the Spirit is walking in the rhythm of God set by the heartbeat of God.

THIRTEEN REVOLUTIONARY WORDS

Jesus is the heartbeat of God! His sinless life now dwells in you. His substitutionary and sacrificial death *as* you on the cross loosed you from every bondage and chain that once strangled your life. His supernatural resurrection empowers you to walk with every breath in newness of life—His divine life. His sovereign ascension releases His authority now. Authority that *commands* you to go!

The mandate from our resurrected Lord is clear, concise, and not up for negotiation. He commands *every* follower to "go into all the world and preach the good news to all creation."[46] These thirteen words burn inside me. Do you seek a word from the Lord? Here it is. Here is *His* will for your life. Here is His direction for you. Go! Every person breathing in this generation is our opportunity, our open door.

> **Do you seek a word from the Lord? Here is His direction for you. Go! Every person breathing in this generation is our opportunity, our open door.**

Moody held a month-long student conference. The bold challenge was all should go and go to all. Night after night the students sought God in prayer. One hundred students committed themselves to go into the entire world. As the wind of God continued to breathe on this movement, thousands followed Jesus to distant places to make *His* name famous!

MANDATE

We must go into the entire world because of the blood of Christ. Men without Christ are condemned. Millions right now live in the shadow of death without a preacher and without the written Word of God. The

---

[46] Mark 16:15

blood of Jesus is the *only* way into a right relationship with God. His dripping blood is the eternal evidence of His unconditional love.

We must go into the entire world because of the blood of the martyrs. Being a disciple of Jesus demands all. Thousands of miles of the harvest field have never felt the footsteps of one sower. Christianity without sacrifice is counterfeit Christianity. Christianity without persecution is sterile Christianity. Christianity without passion for Christ that results in *personal* action to take His love to those who have never heard is no Christianity at all. Many people do not obey the *direct* command of Jesus to *go* because they have not responded to His invitation to *come* to Him!

Many people do not obey the direct command of Jesus to go because they have not responded to His invitation to come to Him!

To know Jesus, by personal experience, is to be filled with His burning heart and His passion. We are in the lineage of those who paid the price in Spirit-led supplication and sacrificial selflessness. We are in the lineage of the prophets of God who dared to speak in His name and were executed. Their voices will never be chained. Their voices will never be silenced!

Preachers will make pulpits famous. Prophets make prisons famous. They are devoted to Jesus and have counted the cost. They rejoice when counted worthy to suffer for His name. They commune with Him in the dark prison cells of torture in cities hostile to the Gospel. They are laid-down lovers.

Father God formed you in the womb so millions who have never heard the message of hope through the life and sacrifice of Jesus will hear in this generation!

Do you want to understand why God marked your life? God wants you to know Him intimately and He has a unique assignment for you. *He* is sending you to the millions who have never picked up a New Testament in their language. Children, students, fathers who have never heard the voice of a follower of Jesus speak to them in person. Father God formed you in the womb so millions who have never heard the message of hope through the life and sacrifice of Jesus will *hear* in this generation!

We must go into the entire world because the blood of sinners is on the hands of the watchmen. Christ's mandate is not negotiable. Jesus said, "As the Father has sent me, I am sending you."[47] He

---

[47] John 20:21

made it clear that this Gospel of the Kingdom will be preached in the entire world as a testimony to every people group.

The follower of Jesus must never be lured by the deception that they can commit the eternal destiny of the lost to the next generation of believers. So many have committed their finances to projects of self-indulgence while thousands go enslaved into eternal death.

The light that obliterates the darkness of a devil's hell for millions is the blazing fire of Pentecost. You are filled with the Holy Ghost to *be empowered* as a witness to every nation. How can a church fulfill their mission when the pastor is not weeping over the lost? How can I expect to fulfill my God-designed

The light that obliterates the darkness of a devil's hell for millions is the blazing fire of Pentecost.

destiny if I neglect the millions outside of my own country who have never heard the name of Jesus?

Jesus got up while it was still dark. He left the house where He was staying. He sat with His Father, listening to His voice and receiving His direction. When His disciples found Him, they were frustrated because of all the people waiting to see Him. Jesus knew the heartbeat of His Father. He was resolute. We *must* go to other cities also for that is why *I was sent!*

You were given *one candle of life.* Burn in the dark and distant places. Burn where people are dying in darkness and not in a land flooded with light. Flirt with the deadly attractions of this polluted world if you desire. Pitch your tent toward the promiscuity and pomp of Sodom. The burning ones will go into *all the world* and preach this Gospel to *every* person. We will fulfill the purpose for which God *marked us!*

The burning ones will go into all the world and preach this Gospel to every person. We will fulfill the purpose for which God marked us!

Nazareth didn't know it. Jerusalem didn't know it. Rome didn't know it. You can *deny* but you can *never destroy* the church of the Lord Jesus Christ! We have a mighty baptism of fire. People cower in panic that the terrorists are coming. I tell you the day will come when marching foot will join marching foot. The beating of the drums will be in perfect cadence. There will be one banner. One Commander!

The burning ones are coming as flames of fire. Overflowing with supernatural love, we will fill every nation of this earth. Christ is coming! This is our moment!

THE RELEASED LIFE

How will this be accomplished? Partnership! There is a supernatural partnership in the Gospel. The Holy Spirit calls and marks you for a specific assignment. He will align you with others to represent His name together in the earth.

I have a vision from God burning deep inside of me. I see men running in sync with the Holy Spirit into the nations of the earth. God's heart is not one man fulfilling a dream alone. Men running together. Families united by the Spirit living Antioch in our generation. We clearly expect signs and wonders to confirm the Word of God. Our hearts are marked and we are willing to pay any price!

The Holy Spirit will align you with others to represent His name together in the earth.

The Great Commission is *not* the beginning of God's plan for the nations. Before the creation of this world, there is a Lamb that was slain for every person living on this earth. Jesus is that Lamb and He said, "The wind blows wherever it pleases. You hear its sound—but you cannot tell where it comes from or where it is going. So it is with everyone born of the Spirit."[48]

---

[48] John 3:8

The Antioch church in Syria is the first time in the New Testament there is intentionality to go to frontier regions to plant new assemblies of Christ followers. We are called to live this Antioch-released life in partnership with the Holy Spirit!

PROPHETS AND TEACHERS

"Now in the church at Antioch there were prophets and teachers: Barnabas, Simeon called Niger, Lucius of Cyrene, Manaen (who had been brought up with Herod the tetrarch) and Saul."[49] We are living *from* an identity—not working to get an identity! When we sit with Jesus and walk in rhythm with His heartbeat, we are drawn to others and supernaturally aligned to serve Him in partnership in our generation.

Men did not vote these leaders in Antioch in. They were not striving to make a name for themselves. They were not cursed by a busy yet barren life. They were free from the slave master's voice that drives a man to work harder to accomplish more to establish an identity.

No, burning ones live *from* an identity. We belong to Jesus. I am His! Loving Him is enough for me. Laying down my life in obedience to Him is my singular delight and desire. Identity creates your sphere of influence and activity. When we burn for Him, people

---

[49] Acts 13:1

will hear *the Voice* in your voice. It is Jesus speaking. It is a move of God—your face radiant with His glory.

If I see Jesus inaccurately, then it is impossible for me to know myself completely. Prophets and teachers burning for God can only lead in unity when they are immersed in the life and identity of Jesus. These prophetic brothers, declaring the Word of the Lord together, reveal the New Testament blueprint of church government.

When we burn for Him, people will hear the Voice in your voice. It is Jesus speaking. It is a move of God— your face radiant with His glory.

It is not normal to elect one man to serve as a pastor. Not one church in the New Testament functioned in this way. We say with our lips that we are committed to the Word of God, yet our traditions bind and choke the life of God out of most congregations. Prophets declare the mind of God. They strengthen, encourage, and comfort with conviction. Their message is Jesus speaking His Word in season.

The Holy Spirit directs Luke to document the names of this leadership team that changed the world to emphasize the heart of God. These men came from all classes of society, were from multiple ethnicities, and were completely united.

TRADITIONS THAT CHOKE

One hundred twenty Christ followers were fervently praying when Jesus immersed them into the Holy Ghost and fire. Within months, there were over 15,000 followers of Jesus in Jerusalem. What a move of God! Yet the majority was Jewish. The Jewish law forbade eating with Gentiles and condemned even entering the home of a Gentile.

They were filled with faith and were meeting together every day. They proclaimed that Jesus was the only name by which men must be saved and yet were only taking the Gospel to people who were *just like them*. Having heard the Great Commission did not get them out of their secure and predictable world. Persecution thrust them into all the earth!

When Stephen laid down his life, Jesus stood up. The church was scattered. Those who left Jerusalem and traveled three hundred miles north to reach this major city in Syria would impact Antioch. The first preachers of the Gospel in Antioch, however, went only to the Jewish community. In the Mediterranean world of that time, there were six million Jews and over 244 million Gentiles. God's heartbeat is that no one would perish but that all would come to repentance and new life in His Son.

Traditions choke. Traditions blind. Traditions chain people. One encounter with the resurrected

Jesus breaks all of that off of you and fills your heart with God's intense love for *all* nations. You dance in freedom. Your every footstep is now in cadence with His Spirit!

Barnabas was Jewish. God used him in the natal days of Saul's walk with God. He was a man who understood the grace of God and gave himself freely to build up others.

Simeon was born in a Jewish family and married an African. Many students of the Gospel believe he was the man who was forced to carry the cross of Jesus.

Lucius was from North Africa. Manaen is another living miracle called to lead on this prophetic team. He was the foster brother of Herod Antipas who murdered John the Baptizer. Luke emphasizes that he grew up in the palace. So how did he encounter Jesus? This man came to Christ by John's influence!

You can chain the man of God. You can *never* silence his voice and influence for the Kingdom of God. Even while chained in the dungeon of Herod's lavish palace, John continued to proclaim Jesus. Manaen, transformed and filled with the Spirit, is a vital leader in Antioch.

Prophets give their lives. The voice of God in them continues to speak in every generation. Saul, radically transformed in one encounter with Jesus, now leads in this ministry to all nations.

FIRST MINISTRY

"While they were worshiping the Lord and fasting, the Holy Spirit said, 'Set apart for me Barnabas and Saul for the work to which I have called them.'"[50] This dynamic house church understood first ministry. These families placed priority on ministering *to* Jesus.

Ruthlessly cut out every activity in your life that God's voice did not set in motion!

The anointing always is strongest when we are singing *to* Him—not just about Him or about us.

I am so jealous to listen and hear clearly the voice of God's precious Holy Spirit. No movement or action took place *until* they heard the voice of God. Ruthlessly cut out every activity in your life that God's voice did not set in motion!

Saul and Barnabas were all in—worshiping, going after Jesus. Their call was already inside of them. Walking in freedom, they had no compulsion to manipulate their way into a position. Their first ministry was *Him*. The timing of their release into apostolic ministry belonged to God. They would not go alone. Saul and Barnabas together with the Spirit of God were about to launch an entirely new movement!

---

[50] Acts 13:2

Jesus will always stand up in men who have died to themselves. "I have been crucified with Christ and I no longer live, but Christ lives in me. The life I live in the body, I live by faith in the Son of God, who loved me and gave Himself for me."[51] The portal into depth, substance, and reality in walking with Jesus is death—complete surrender. Yield yourself to Him and you will be astounded as Jesus begins to live every moment in you.

> **The portal into depth, substance, and reality in walking with Jesus is death—complete surrender.**

THE VOICE OF THE HOLY SPIRIT

"While they were worshiping the Lord and fasting, the Holy Spirit said, 'Set apart for me Barnabas and Saul for the work to which I have called them.' So after they had fasted and prayed, they placed their hands on them and sent them off."[52]

This is *normal* church. This is what the Kingdom of God on earth looks like. This is moving at the directive of the Holy Spirit. I live for this! I dream of this! I burn with this vision inside of me. I lead with Jesus out in front and follow Him into this reality!

---

[51] Gal. 2:20
[52] Acts 13:2-4

In an atmosphere of public worship, intentional fasting, and united devotion to Jesus, the Holy Spirit's

The Spirit of God speaks to the entire body to release those He has already called.

voice will be active. He commands! Set apart *for Me!* It is an imperative, strong demand.

When did we embrace the lie that we can follow Jesus and choose our own way? Where did we get the idea that it was normal for a church to exist only to pacify carnal, self-absorbed members? There is a burning fire that is breaking into the hearts of those in love with Jesus. The Spirit of God speaks to the entire body to release those *He* has already called. This is normal. This is life. I will not live any other way!

The Antioch church fasted and prayed further. Then, they placed their hands on them. Jacob imparted blessing to his grandsons, crossing his arms when he laid his hands on them. The entire community laying hands on them commissioned the Levites. Joshua was filled with the spirit of wisdom as Moses laid his hands on him. Elisha, the prophet, put his hands on the king's hands and authority for victory over the Lord's enemies was imparted.

Jesus laid His hands on bruised and brokenhearted people to release physical healing. He placed His hands on children and blessed them. Multitudes hungry for

God were baptized in the Holy Spirit as Peter and John placed their hands on them and a city was transformed. Timothy received a definite spiritual gift through the laying on of hands.

Now in Syria, in direct and immediate obedience to the Holy Spirit, the church places their hands on Barnabas and Saul to release them, to set them free to proclaim Jesus to millions that had never heard the message. The Holy Spirit sends them on their way. As they went, the Holy Spirit went with them.

When Jesus is everything to you He will empower you to bring eternal change everywhere He sends you.

The released life is one of continual communion with the Holy Spirit. It is yielding to His voice. When Jesus is everything to you He will empower you to bring eternal change *everywhere* He sends you. When this specific assignment is completed, the Spirit leads these men back to Antioch.

The Holy Spirit is still speaking. He is still calling men and women to experience Jesus and be the expression of Jesus to multiplied millions who have never heard His name. The authority to go is in the commission of Jesus. The empowering comes in our personal encounter with Him. God is still opening the door of faith. He has marked you by design to release you!

6

Impostors

⟨ornament⟩

"I was born to fight devils and factions. It is
my business to remove obstacles, to cut down
thorns, to open and make straight paths. If I
must have some failing let me rather speak the
truth with too great sincerity than once to act
the hypocrite and conceal the truth."
—Martin Luther[53]

God chose the weak to shame the strong. God
chose to place His apostles at the end of the
procession. They are the least among the prisoners of
war. They are not in the procession of the affluent

---

[53] Martin Luther, "Favorite Quotes," *The Gospel Writer*, http://
thegospelwriter.com/favorite-quotes/.

and powerful. They stand with those condemned to a public death.

The Father watched His Son brutally murdered to reconcile you back to Himself. The Son, by a decision of His will, laid down His life. The ransom for my release from eternal death was His extravagant love. His love looked like weakness to the world. Jesus embraced dishonor, cursing, and torture at the hands of finite beings He created to demonstrate the wisdom of God and identify with you.

As a Jesus preacher living in Shanghai, the biblical word "apostle" came alive to me. From my childhood, it was my understanding that missionaries are the sent ones. They are the apostles of this present generation.

It is quite evident, however, that many living overseas were not at all apostles as defined in the New Testament. Jesus was sent by His Father. He sacrificed. He learned obedience through what He suffered. His every action was directed by the voice of His Father.

APOSTOLIC MORNINGS

"Very early in the morning, while it was still dark, Jesus got up, left the house and went off to a solitary place, where he prayed."[54] This is the heart and foundation of all apostolic ministries. The burning desire to be alone with the Father is what marks the

---

[54] Mark 1:35

life of everyone authentically called by God without exception.

Very early. While it was still dark. The Spirit of God makes this *very* clear. Jesus got up…a decision of His will. Left the house…the demands and distractions of multiple voices. His life was directed by *one* voice. His heart belonged to His Father. In that solitary place of stillness, He prayed.

The burning desire to be alone with the Father is what marks the life of everyone authentically called by God without exception.

Some of the strongest prayers are never words. It is *being* with the one we love.

Leaders incessantly talk about techniques and strategies for transforming the world. God wants to speak with you *alone*.

Men always substitute action and busyness in an attempt to camouflage their lack of direction from the heart of the Father. "Let the majority vote. This reveals the heart of God." What could be more nonsensical than adhering to that traditional thinking? God speaks. The Father has a purpose. God delights in revealing Himself to those hungering and thirsting for Him.

The majority is often wrong…very wrong. The self-reliant will never pray. The self-important sense no need for hours with their Father. The self-righteous run right past Him on their way to working "for Him."

Jesus was asked, what must we *do* in order to inherit eternal life…what must we *do* in order to accomplish the works God requires? "The work of God is this: to believe in the one he has sent" was the response of Jesus.[55] Then they asked for a sign from Him in order to ignite faith in their hearts. "Those with a 'works' mentality will always watch for God to *work* for them. "What will You *do?*" they ask. "What will You *give?*" they ask.

When being with Jesus is not enough, we will always attempt to supplement His presence with His actions.

Being with Jesus was not enough. When being with Jesus is not enough, we will always attempt to supplement His presence with His actions.[56] Jesus continues in this confrontation to declare, "I am the bread of life. He who comes to me will never go hungry, and he who believes in me will never be thirsty."[57] The answer is to come to Him. The burning desire *in you* can only be satisfied *in Him.*

Jesus is in that place of stillness when Peter and his companions rush in. Mark's gospel describes it this

---

[55] John 6:29
[56] Michael Dow text message, Feb. 7, 2015.
[57] John 6:35

way, "When they found him, they exclaimed: 'Everyone is looking for you!'"[58] *"Everyone* needs you *now!"* they *exclaimed!* The disciples and the crowds always make demands. *Exclamation point!* It is the dictatorship of the *urgent.* The *rush* of the majority. It is the constant voice driven by the appetites of those who will not stop to listen to the Father for themselves.

Jesus was *sent* by His Father. Authentic apostles are sent by God, centered in God, and directed by only one voice—the voice of God. As the Father has sent Him, Jesus right now sends you. Don't rush past this. You can't accomplish anything if you design and pattern your life on anyone other than Jesus. Jesus, very early, left the house and was alone with His Father.

The answer is to come to Him. The burning desire in you can only be satisfied in Him.

No counterfeit "devotional" will cut it in the thick of the battle to rescue men and women from the darkness of hell. The gates of the enemy do not crash when approached by pseudo-apostles wearing masks pretending to be the real deal.

The clear, cutting response of Jesus is so powerful. "Let us go somewhere else—to the nearby cities—so I can preach there also. That is why I have come."[59]

[58] Mark 1:37
[59] Mark 1:38

Jesus continues moving forward, traveling throughout
Galilee. As He is listening to His Father, He continues
preaching and driving out demons. Jesus is powerful
in word and action. The kingdom of evil cannot stand
in His presence!

The morning is the birthing point of my day. It
is very early in the morning when I sit with Jesus. It
is there in His beautiful gaze that directives for the
day come...His design for who to speak with, how to
align each moment of the day as it awakens, who to
call, what to say an emphatic *no* to; when to go, when
to be still.

Tragically, many ministers of the Gospel jump out
of their bed directly into the demands of the disciples
and the crowds. They have no joy and see zero effec-
tiveness because they cannot discern the rhythm of
God. They dance every day to the relentless pulsating
beat played by those *they have placed* as gods in their lives.

They yearn to hear the rhythm of Pentecost. Their
hearts crave Him, in that deep private place, but they
are unwilling to break free from the deadening melody
that has held them captive for so many years.

WILDERNESS FIRE

Apostles moving in the power of the Holy Ghost
will rescue millions who have never heard the name of
Jesus. Those who discern the voice of God know they
are sent to everyone that does not know Jesus in every

nation. No impostors, pretenders, impersonators, masqueraders, imitators. Jesus exposed the impostors of His day.[60] He said these pseudo-religious leaders:

- did not practice what they preached;
- did everything for show/for the attention of men;
- loved to be served.

God, examine my heart. Let me die to myself. You are so ready to introduce and send your dead men into the world. Empower me. Fill me now!

It's time to strip off the masks and to align ourselves with true, authentic apostles who burn to see the name of Jesus famous throughout every nation of the earth. Real apostles are formed in the fire of the wilderness!

"I will keep on doing what I am doing in order to cut the ground from under those who want an opportunity to be considered equal with us in the things they boast about. For such men are false apostles, deceitful workmen, masquerading as apostles of Christ."[61]

Jesus used these words, written by Paul, to completely wreck my life as a young missionary in my twenties living in Asia. My God, I never want to masquerade as a man of God! Jesus is King. He

---

[60] Matt. 23
[61] 2 Cor. 11:12-13

demands complete allegiance. His voice is majestic. He rules with authority. His voice has unlimited power. *That very* voice released His commission to preach and demonstrate His Kingdom. We will see heaven invade earth in our generation as we obey His voice!

You either bear the scars of Jesus on your body or you will wear a mask to pretend you are His.

God is looking for the weak. He desires those who have no confidence in their own strength. When God marks a man to be His voice, He will send him into the wilderness. Moses. David. John the Baptizer. Jesus. Paul. They all carry the scars of the wilderness. They were all formed in the fire of the wilderness. The Spirit of the Living God led them there. You either bear the scars of Jesus on your body or you will wear a mask to pretend you are *His*.

Moses was pulled out of the water. He was trained in the language, mentality, and culture of the mighty Egyptian empire. He was adorned in the wardrobe of nobility and had his every desire catered to immediately. As an adult, he was pulled toward his purpose— to be a deliverer. God wanted to deliver a nation through him. Moses sensed it. As an eyewitness to injustice, he was angered and immediately stepped into action. His impulsive response banished him to forty years, stripped of everything royal.

Then God comes to him in the wilderness. God is not afraid of the wilderness, you know. He does not fear the cacophony of wild screams from untamed beasts. The poisonous sting of deadly vipers does not alarm Him. He comes to you in your wilderness. In that ordinary shrub, fire burns. Our God is a consuming fire! The fire of God's presence burns. The voice of the Almighty speaks. God has nothing to do with frauds, impostors, and mask wearers. He comes to the broken. He comes to those with scars. He *only* comes to those who know they are nothing.

You may dream of transforming the nations. You will not see it until you have walked through the fire of the wilderness. Your heart burns to preach, to see every sick person healed, to command the dead to be raised to life. You must see the fire first. You must encounter the God of the burning bush. You must let go and be stripped of all that the palace gave you. The pride, the selfish ambition, the desire for your name to be known...you must die to it all in the wilderness.

God comes to those with scars. He only comes to those who know they are nothing.

And then *suddenly* He comes. He has been watching over every moment in that wilderness. He protected you, cared for you, sang over you, loved you, dreamed of you...and now it's time. The time has come. The fire is burning. It will touch you. He is here! God is standing right in front of you.

He calls. He has heard the millions in their misery and suffering. God has come down to deliver, to release, to loose! He is looking for that man that He marked. The years in the palace were not wasted. No, emphatically, no…not one moment was wasted.

He comes…only to those who no longer feel they can speak. They have died to their dream. Their dreams of delivering millions have been crushed.

He cannot use a man full of himself. His voice will not speak through one who is enamored with his own voice. Oh, He comes…only to those who no longer feel they can speak. They have died to their dream. Their dreams of delivering millions have been crushed. It all seems too distant, too painful.

And then the fire burns! The fire of His presence comes. He speaks. The silence is over. The pain is raw. He confronts. He assigns. He sends. He rips off the mask and you are trying to hide what is underneath. You are unwilling for anyone to see those scars.

Oh, if only He had sent you when you were in the palace. If only that man could have been His voice. No, the fire of anonymity, the loneliness of the desert, the deadening routine of the sheep; it is all part of His process. Honor the process of Jesus in your life. Now He sends you!

Moses...I am *sending you*. Moses says he can't speak. Moses asks God to choose someone else. Moses is so desperate to get out of this mandate that he inquires, "What if they do not believe me or listen to me and say, 'The Lord did not appear to you'?"[62] The Lord immediately responds with a question. "What is that in your hand?" Moses says, "A staff."[63]

Truly amazing. The scar. The sign of your decades in isolation...the staff. This is exactly what God is going to use to demonstrate the power of His name. It is this shepherd's staff that Moses will raise and millions of Israelis will march boldly into freedom baptized in the Red Sea. Moses will not hold the scepter of the throne of Egypt to break out a nation. He will hold a despised rugged piece of wood.

Moses will not hold the scepter of the throne of Egypt to break out a nation. He will hold a despised rugged piece of wood.

His life was formed in the fire of the wilderness and the scar of that experience will liberate a nation. Jesus comes directly out of Jordan's waters of baptism and is led into the wilderness by the

[62] Ex. 4:1
[63] Ex. 4:2

Holy Spirit. He is viciously and intentionally attacked by the evil one. He conquers as a man dependent on the Holy Spirit.

Jesus is beaten, mocked, flogged, and nailed to a despised rugged piece of wood. As that wood is lifted high into the heavens, the powers of darkness are broken forevermore. Principalities and powers are stripped of their authority. Moses was sent, the sign of his scars was raised, and national deliverance was birthed. Jesus will forever carry the scars on His hands and His feet. His broken body was raised to release *every nation*.

Your capacity to discern His voice and follow His leading is cultivated and formed in the wilderness.

A great multitude that no one can count from every nation, tribe, people, and language will stand before the throne and in front of this Lamb. In a loud voice they will cry out that salvation belongs to our God, who sits on the throne and to the Lamb.[64] The Lamb who suffered will receive the reward of His suffering. The man sent by God, formed in the fire of the wilderness, speaks life and freedom to every nation. It's time to see millions break out into eternal freedom.

---

[64] Rev. 7:9

David, anointed to be king, runs as a fugitive into the wilderness trying to escape the snares of death. God's sent ones are not impostors. There is a price to be paid. Your capacity to discern His voice and follow His leading is cultivated and formed in the wilderness.

Songs were birthed in the heart of David as he hid in caves and ran across barren heights. Surrounded by thousands of enemies, he learned to trust God and to run in rhythm to God's heartbeat. David ascends to the throne. He reigns as God promised. Jesus, the Royal Son and true Son of David, will reign forever!

MASQUERADING

How can we distinguish the authentic apostle from those who are just assuming an identity? How are apostles marked by design? Apostles wage war with divine power. "For though we live in

Apostles wage war with divine power.

the world, we do not wage war as the world does. The weapons we fight with are not the weapons of the world. On the contrary, they have divine power to demolish strongholds. We demolish arguments and every pretension that sets itself up against the knowledge of God, and we take captive every thought to make it obedient to Christ."[65]

---

[65] 2 Cor. 10:3-5

Apostles are Spirit filled and Spirit led. Their assignments are directed by the voice of the Holy Spirit Himself. You can study every model of leadership in the world. You can fly from nation to nation to witness ministries in person. You will never rise above death and the status quo unless you walk with God fully, completely, and breath by breath. Treasure His voice!

Alex Buchan, who served as bureau chief for Compass Direct, writes about his encounters with Chinese leader Wang Ming-Dao:

> The first time I met him he asked, "Young man, how do you walk with God?" I listed disciplines I practiced like Bible study and prayer, to which he retorted, "Wrong answer…to walk with God you must go at walking pace."
>
> I had no idea what he meant. The next time I encountered him I asked about his twenty-three-year prison experience. Wang Ming-Dao asked, "When you go back home, how many books do you have to read, how many letters to write, messages to preach? He stopped me as I tried to answer and said, "You need to build yourself a cell."
>
> He explained, "When I was put in jail I was devastated. I was an evangelist. I wanted to hold crusades all over China. I was an author.

I wanted to write books. I was a preacher. I wanted to study my Bible and write sermons. But I had no Bible, no pulpit, no audience, no pen and paper. I could do nothing. Nothing except get to know God. And for twenty years that was the greatest relationship I have ever known. But the cell was the means. I was pushed into a cell, but you will have to push yourself into one. Simplify your life, so you have time to know God."[66]

The suffering church understands that to walk with God you must sit with Him. Listen to Him. Enjoy Him! We can only wage war with divine weapons. Strongholds, arguments, pretensions, and deceptions can only be broken in the authority of King Jesus. Apostles are people of power. This empowering is the Holy Spirit Himself living within us and directing us.

RAZOR-SHARP FOCUS

Apostles preach Jesus where He has never been preached before. "Neither do we go beyond our limits by boasting of work done by others. Our hope is that, as your faith continues to grow, our area of acting

---

[66] I discovered this article many years ago in a magazine concerning ministry in Asia. I had included it in an annual report I wrote while living in China.

among you will greatly expand, so that we can preach the gospel in the regions beyond you."[67] Paul is very

Apostles preach Jesus where He has never been preached before.

clear concerning his identity as a true apostle of Jesus. "It has always been my ambition to preach the gospel where Christ was not known, so that I would not be building on someone else's foundation."[68] All evangelism is not equal. Paul has priorities that are mandated in his call to apostolic ministry.

All people are equally lost without Christ. All people do not have equal *access* to the Gospel. Apostolic teams were sent from Antioch in Syria, by the direct imperative of the Spirit, to pioneer and plant new assemblies of believers where the message of Jesus was being preached for the first time.

China is home to over 230 cities of one million people or more. North America represents seven percent of the global world population. There are more people currently alive in Asia than in the rest of the world combined. America must be saved. We are expecting a great awakening in this nation.

We also hear the call of the Spirit of God to *every* nation. Those who currently have *no access* to the

---

[67] 2 Cor. 10:15-16
[68] Rom. 15:20

Gospel are going to hear in our generation. You were marked by design for this very purpose. This is our time. The apostles are coming!

A conversation with two leaders of house churches in mainland China marked my life forever. They had influence with thousands of Chinese believers. As we sat at a table together in Shanghai, they made no demands. They were desperate for anything we could do to come alongside of them. How my heart was moved! My spirit is still stirred to this very day. Millions and millions of children and students who have never heard the name of Jesus.

All people are equally lost without Christ. All people do not have equal access to the Gospel.

We must hear the voice of our Father and we must *be His voice* to every person alive today!

Reinhard Bonnke got it right: If you go fishing in a bathtub, all you are going to catch is soap! I will never be convinced that God is calling the majority of preachers today to cities in countries that already have thousands of believers and access to Christian books, radio, and television. Is God really silent concerning the millions that have never heard the Gospel?

Apostles are ordinary people who know God's heart and live Jesus in the dark and distant places. They are the burning ones prophesied in the Word of

God coming in the last hours of time. They burn with ambition to know Christ…and to demonstrate His love…*not* building on another man's foundation.

We must hear the voice of our Father and we must be His voice to every person alive today!

God is a master strategist. The two billion people in China and India cry out for cross-cultural messengers to take the water of life to those dying of thirst. The millions across the Middle East will not perish. This generation is filled with the Spirit and burning with His message. The Holy Spirit will not be denied!

"I myself am convinced, my brothers, that you yourselves are full of goodness, complete in knowledge and competent to instruct one another. I have written you quite boldly on some points, as if to remind you of them again because of the grace God gave me to be a minister of Christ Jesus to the Gentiles with the priestly duty of proclaiming the gospel of God, so that the Gentiles might become an offering acceptable to God, sanctified by the Holy Spirit."[69]

Paul has razor-sharp focus. Jesus encountered him, marked his life with a *priestly duty*…the divine responsibility…to proclaim Jesus. There is an offering

---

[69] Rom. 15:14-16

we are called upon to present to God. Our Father desires millions and millions of people lost right now. Our vision sees them becoming an offering acceptable to God. Christ reveals Himself to them and they are offered to God.

This is why I breathe. This is the call that marks my life. Encounter Jesus in this text. Hear the call of the Spirit. See the millions He desires to reveal Himself to right now. Go! Extravagantly, sacrificially give! Your life. Your gifts. Your all. Lay it before Jesus. All of you. The offering of your life so that the nations become an offering acceptable to God!

Hear the call of the Spirit. See the millions He desires to reveal Himself to right now. Go! Extravagantly, sacrificially give!

"Therefore, I glory in Christ Jesus in my service to God. I will not venture to speak anything except what Christ has accomplished through me in leading the Gentiles to obey God by what I have said and done—by the power of signs, and miracles through the power of the Holy Spirit. So from Jerusalem all the way around to Illyricum, I have fully proclaimed the gospel of Christ. It has always been my ambition to preach the gospel where Christ was not known, so that I would not be building on someone else's foundation. Rather, as it is written:

'Those who were not told about him will see, and those who have never heard will understand.'"[70]

Paul was immersed in Isaiah. His quotation from Isaiah 52:15 is branded on my heart. God is calling you to preach where no one has preached before. Jesus endured the cross. He was rejected and despised by men to purchase our freedom. We merged with Him in baptism and His resurrection life is in us now.

Apostles participate in Christ's suffering. The river of blood always precedes the river of anointing.

We live continually being filled with His Spirit *for this reason*...to know Jesus and to be God carriers to the nations. Don't settle. Stop fishing in the bathtub. Make His name famous in the earth. The suffering servant, the Lamb slain will receive *His reward!*

KINGS CARRY CROSSES

Apostles participate in Christ's suffering. Paul was not an impostor. His documentation of credentials detail privations, perils, and persecution. The river of blood always precedes the river of anointing. When Judas, possessed by the evil one, went out to betray

---

[70] Rom. 15:17-21

Jesus, our Lord said, "Now is the Son of Man glorified and God is glorified in him."[71]

Paul said, "We are like men condemned to die in the arena: We are weak, go hungry, and thirsty, are in rags, are brutally treated, are homeless, we work hard with our own hands. When we are cursed, we bless; when we are persecuted, we endure it; when we are slandered, we answer kindly."[72] There are more believers in prison in mainland China than any other country in our world. Apostles who daily face fines and execution challenge the no-risk atmosphere of soft Christianity.

Apostles who daily face fines and execution challenge the no-risk atmosphere of soft Christianity.

Why were you born? It was not to experience a life of ease while millions go into eternity without Christ. Get out of your self-imposed prison of security! Sleepless nights, danger, lashes, pressure… these are the marks of Christ followers!

Until I understand the purpose for which God formed me in the womb, I will never have God's perspective on my time, my resources, and my destiny. Knowing God's purpose for my life and abandoning myself to Jesus completely, I stand strong despite

[71] John 13:31
[72] 1 Cor. 4:9-13

every force of hell fighting against me. I can stand when those who have pledged their allegiance to mammon ridicule me. I am unmoved when mocked by those who say there is more important work than taking the Gospel to the regions beyond.

Knowing God's purpose for my life and abandoning myself to Jesus completely, I stand strong despite every force of hell fighting against me.

I want to know Jesus! I want to know Him in the power of His resurrection and I want to share in the fellowship of His sufferings. I want to be considered worthy to suffer for His name. Apostles bleed. Apostles are marked. Apostles *participate* in the current sufferings of Jesus Christ.

He is not far off on His throne watching us suffer. The Son of the Most High abides in us. We are dead. He lives in us. He *present tense* suffers and we commune with Him and participate in that fellowship that is filled with glory!

"I have worked much harder, been in prison more frequently, been flogged more severely, and been exposed to death again and again. Five times I received from the Jews the forty lashes minus one. Three times I was beaten with rods, once I was stoned, three times I was shipwrecked. I spent a night and a day in the open sea. I have been constantly on the move. I have been in danger from rivers, in danger from bandits, in danger in the country, in danger at sea, and in danger from false brothers. I have labored and toiled and have often gone without sleep; I have known hunger and thirst and have often gone without food; I have been cold and naked. Besides everything else, I face daily the pressure of my concern for all the churches."[73]

Bonhoeffer said: "The Christian belongs not in the seclusion of a cloistered life but in the thick of foes."[74] He lived for Jesus. He gave his life. Jesus is sending you out into the thick of foes. Be a God carrier. Never look back. Focus your eyes on Jesus!

What's behind the mask? Look for the evidence of true apostleship. Suffering. God will place the wood upon you. Deny yourself. Lay your life down. Carry your cross! Dr. Bob Gladstone is right: Kings always carry crosses in God's Kingdom!

AMBASSADORS WITH AUTHORITY

"The things that mark an apostle—signs, wonders and miracles—were done among you with great perseverance."[75] Apostles demonstrate the

[73] 2 Cor. 11:23-28

[74] Dietrich Bonhoeffer, "Dietrich Bonhoeffer Quotes," *goodreads*, http://www.goodreads.com/quotes/316815-jesus-christ-lived-in-the-midst-of-his-enemies-at.

[75] 2 Cor. 12:12

supernatural power of God. If you strip away the mask, many living overseas as missionaries are lacking this vital dimension of supernatural power.

Apostles demonstrate the supernatural power of God.

The challenge of reaching those in the most distant places in this generation is *not* the darkness…it is the absence of light. Ambassadors with authority are feared in hell. Signs, wonders, and miracles done with *great perseverance*. Apostle, stay until Jesus is known and His church is established!

It was my honor over twenty years ago to participate in the crusade in Mongolia that resulted in hundreds coming to Christ. It is such a privilege to be an eyewitness to a nation opening up to the Gospel. The newly planted church almost immediately started a Bible school to train nationals to lead this new movement. So many young adults that were deaf were instantly healed. The worship of these brand new followers of Jesus is still alive inside of me.

During the ministry time, a monk stepped to the front of the auditorium during one of the evening meetings trying to disrupt people who were coming to Christ. One of the Chinese believers from Hong Kong that was there in the meeting understood the nature of this warfare. This businessman quietly spoke with authority: "I bind you in the name of Jesus."

I was right there. I was playing the keyboard on the platform inches away from this encounter. That monk was unable to speak, or move, or disrupt the meeting in any way. There is power in the name of Jesus! There is no other name that can break the chains of slavery to sin and destroy the fear of death.

The blind see. The lame walk. We have seen brain cancer vanish in Jesus' name. The dead are raised. In China, a four-year-old boy drowned. His body was laid in the middle room of the house. Christ followers went into fervent prayer. They heard a shout, "Come and see!" They were told, "When you shouted 'Jesus!' a man in bright, white clothes placed his hand on the child's head. The boy is alive!" Those who were perishing in darkness enter into eternal life!

The burning ones consider no risk too great in order to be able to participate in Christ's suffering.

Where are the apostles? Where are those who will walk with God? Where are those who are willing to live among the nations in the difficult places? Where are those men and women willing to suffer all for the name of Christ? The burning ones consider no risk too great in order to be able to participate in Christ's suffering. Where are those demonstrating God's supernatural power?

They are the children living in our homes. They are the students desperate to know why they were born into this world. They are the ordinary people seeking God at our altars that God will use in extraordinary ways.

Go where the church does not exist. Run with Jesus into the nations!

God is speaking to you today. Surrender to Him. Encounter Him. Kneel right where you are. You are in His presence! That's His voice speaking to you. Go where the church does not exist. Run with Jesus into the nations!

7

Branded

I bear the branded marks of Jesus on my body.
—Galatians 6:17

Jesus comes to you to brand you forever. His desire is to permanently brand you right now with the Holy Ghost and with fire. I am not inviting you into a denominational definition of Spirit immersion. I am calling you to a fire branding by your Lord.

This is not about having a one-time historical experience of speaking in tongues. This call is to, present tense, continual immersion into fire to be His witness with your every breath. Every place your feet step, heaven is invading earth!

He is ready to mark you right now. Paul, the laid-down lover of Jesus, had his heart torn open witnessing the first generation of Christ followers in the region of Galatia move away from pure devotion to Christ Himself.

"Those who want to make a good impression outwardly are trying to compel you to be circumcised. The only reason they do this is to avoid being persecuted for the cross of Christ. Not even those who are circumcised obey the Law, yet they want you to be circumcised that they may boast about your flesh. May I never boast except in the cross of our Lord Jesus Christ, through which the world has been crucified to me, and I to the world. Finally, let no one cause me trouble, for I bear on my body the marks of Jesus."[76]

Paul, writing here with his own pen dipped in blood and tears, speaks with apostolic authority. He is a marked man. He is branded with the *very wounds* of Jesus Himself!

The Gospel transforms the whole basis of my identity. Nothing in this world has *any* power over me. I am not inferior to anyone or superior to anyone. The leadership of the Holy Ghost in my life is transforming me into someone entirely *new!* Permanent scars inflicted by the hands of enemies are now transformed supernaturally into priceless, beautiful marks of identification.

---

[76] Gal. 6:12-14, 17

Paul is branded with scars marking his oneness with Christ. Branding is the mark of ownership. The greatest lover, Jesus Himself, has branded me with His own life. I no longer live. Jesus breathes in me! His actual, passionate, burning heart is now my heart. The branded marks are the outward evidence of His inward grace empowering me.

Branding is the mark of ownership. The greatest lover, Jesus Himself, has branded me with His own life.

I cannot stand for Him without the power of *His* life burning within me. The allegiance of my entire being is devoted to Him as the Spirit of God continually reveals Jesus to me personally. There are no limits, no boundaries, no confines to the endless revealing of His beauty. The Holy Spirit has an *endless* revelation of Jesus. Do you get that? *Endless.* We will forever be captivated by an ever-greater revelation of His beauty!

Paul encountered Jesus on his zealous, obsessed journey to murder as many Christ followers as he could in one lifetime. His transformation is so radical, so intense, so Jesus, that now *he* bears on his body the wounds of Jesus. The revelation of Jesus to you personally sets you apart as *holy to the Lord.* You have no other master. No passion is stronger than your intense love for Him.

DEFINING MOMENT

Matthew 16 is the *defining moment* word of the Lord that blasted the doorway open for me into an entirely new season of walking intimately with the Holy Spirit. The man God used on November 23, 2014 was Michael Dow. From that moment on everything has been new. This revelation is a doorway. It's a sign inviting you to "run this way" into the presence of Jesus. Knowing, by experience, Jesus as the Royal Son empowers you to endure persecution for His name.

Being cursed, deserted, beaten, forgotten, slandered, and tortured are invitations into intimacy with Jesus. Peter and the other apostles actually overflowed with joy when given the privilege, and they were counted worthy of suffering disgrace for the Name of Jesus.[77] No one could intimidate them. No power could crush their resolve. Jesus Himself branded their burning hearts.

Peter bragged arrogantly before the crucifixion that he would die with Jesus. Peter deserted Jesus. Peter cursed and swore that he did not know Jesus. Once transformed by the Holy Spirit, this Peter *stands* and demonstrates the power of the resurrected Lord. Three thousand lives are instantly transformed as they encounter Jesus!

---

[77] Acts 5:41

In the conversation between Jesus, Peter, and the other disciples recorded for us in Matthew 16, we have the first time Jesus uses the word "church" in the Gospels. Jesus will only speak of the church when there is confession of Him as Christ.

You cannot be lord of your life and proclaim that Jesus is your Savior.

To be branded is to know by revelation *from the Father* that Jesus is the Royal Son. The Kingdom of God is a person. Our identity and purpose, our willingness to suffer for His name, our DNA in the Spirit flows out of this revelation. He is the Royal Son willing to lay down His life, raised in supernatural power, and ascended to His throne giving gifts to men.

It is idolatry to embrace a Jesus that allows you to remain on the throne of your own heart. You cannot be lord of your life and proclaim that Jesus is your Savior. He is Sovereign Royalty. He is King over all! To be in love with Jesus is fatal to your self-addicted life.

Peter is given a revelation of Jesus as Messiah, the Christ. In the deep places of his heart, he still longed for power, for applause, for the authority to rule over others. The branding fire of Jesus burns that out of you. We fall on our faces at His cross. Our hearts are separated from the world and we run with abandon toward Jesus and His desires. We deny ourselves and take up our cross. The fire of Pentecost imparts Him into you. God brands us, marks us so we *become* the message. You are His message in the earth!

God brands us, marks us so we become the message. You are His message in the earth!

Jesus asks His closest followers what the people of that generation were saying about Him. He then goes directly into their hearts. "'Who do you say I am?' Simon Peter answered, 'You are the Christ, the Son of the living God.' Jesus replied, 'Blessed are you, Simon son of Jonah, for this was not revealed to you by man, but by My Father in heaven.'"[78]

Simon son of Jonah. Jesus puts Simon on alert that he is about to change families. This is even more emphatic as Jesus makes clear *My Father* in heaven has revealed this to you. No man can give this revelation to you. We must be born from above. We are immersed into this new family...baptized into the name of the Father, and of the Son, and of the Holy Ghost.

Now let's be clear. We can love and respect people who walk closely with God. We can say to others, "Imitate me as I imitate Christ." Yet the revelation of Jesus that births a desire to live for Him and the

---

[78] Matt. 16:15-17

willingness to die for Him can *only* come from God the Father Himself.

Flesh and blood revelations will never lead you into real satisfaction. Following after a man that is close to God cannot satisfy the deepest longing of your inner man. Only sitting with Jesus, gazing on Jesus, giving the entirety of your being to Jesus will quench that craving within you. The branding comes in this revelation and encounter.

POWER TO STAND

"From that time on Jesus began to explain to His disciples that He must go to Jerusalem, and suffer many things at the hands of the elders, chief priests and teachers of the Law, and that He must be killed and on the third day be raised to life."[79] Transition. New season. New level of conversation. From that time on!

The invitation to follow Jesus demands that we first deny ourselves and take up our cross.

Jesus now invites these men into deeper places of His heart. He came to die. He allows them to see the cup of suffering He is holding in His hand. The call to follow Him is a call to die to your purpose and to experience newness of life—*divine life!*

---

[79] Matt. 16:21

The invitation to follow Jesus demands that we *first* deny ourselves and take up our cross. Peter has a fresh revelation of Jesus; however, he still clings to the entrenched patterns of his natural mind. He refuses to accept that God leads us to experience His glory through absolute sacrifice. No counterfeits. No substitutes. Complete surrender. *Death*. The power to stand with Jesus is birthed only in the man willing to die.

DEATH IN ORLANDO

When God wrecked my world in November 2014, He immediately began to speak to me about certain prophetic demonstrations that I was to walk into obeying Him. These were clear directives. His voice was loving, concise, and very specific.

The Father began to speak to me about the baptism of Jesus and the launching of His ministry of deliverance on the earth. When Jesus stepped into those waters, it was to obey a mandate given to Him by His Father. As a direct result of obedience, Jesus saw the heavens opened. The Spirit of God descended on Him and *remained* on Him. His Father declared His intense love for Jesus and proclaimed to every principality and power Jesus as *His Son*…the promised Royal Son that had come to destroy the works of the enemy.

Jesus spoke to me intimately about Naaman's quest for healing and the directive to be immersed seven times. An Israeli hostage told Naaman's wife that the living God had the power and authority to heal. Naaman expected Elisha, the man of God, to come to him, wave his hand, and then healing would be his. Instead of following Naaman's preconceived idea of how God should heal, Elisha sent a message for Naaman to go completely under the water seven times and he would receive his miracle. Pride, embedded in the heart of this military leader, rejected God's command.

You want to experience the branding of Jesus for real? Die to your demands of how you will receive from God.

The Lord spoke to me about the walls of Jericho falling and the conquest of the *first* city in the fulfillment of taking the entire Promised Land by marching around the city seven times on the seventh day. The power was not in the military strategy; it was in obeying the clear voice of God! Obeying God's directions in Orlando would launch the taking of entire cities for Jesus.

Baptism is merging with Jesus under the water. It is death. It is staying under and being raised in resurrection power. It is union with Jesus. Jesus meets you under the water. It is identification with Jesus. It is the portal into the new breed of laid-down lovers.

You want to experience the branding of Jesus for real? Die to your demands of how you will receive from God. Your tradition, your self-sufficiency, your dependence on your own wisdom is choking miracles out of your life. Listen to the instruction of the Lord and *do it!* Complete obedience releases freedom.

Now for me personally, the journey meant taking a flight to Orlando and driving to the beach the first Sunday of 2015. It meant not giving the instructions, not leading the way, not telling someone else how to do it. I was gut-level honest about what God had placed deep in my spirit. Now it was time to yield to the directive of Jesus Himself.

Listen to the instruction of the Lord and do it! Complete obedience releases freedom.

Michael Dow sent a text the day before Christmas 2014 informing me that: "The beach is happening. The waters of baptism will be a reality. We will inhabit the beach next Sunday morning at the break of day. Jesus will be glorified. Nothing will ever be the same. A new day has dawned. The rising of the *Son* has pierced the darkness and made all things new!"[80] *Yes!*

The result was a supernatural prophetic demonstration that branded my life for eternity. There are eyewitnesses to these events. We arrived at the beach exactly as the sun was rising. We stood with Jesus and

---

[80] Text from Michael Dow, December 24, 2014.

worshiped as the beautiful song *When You Walk into the Room* played. The atmosphere filled with the nearness of Jesus. As we both boldly walked into the water, Michael specifically declared that we were facing east and God was again connecting me to the people He called me to living in the massive cities in Asia.

To my left, the incredible, majestic colors of the sun were dancing on the water. To my right, Michael raised both arms to heaven and began to speak the Word of the Lord. After the first immersion, he began to count each time until the prophetic mandate of seven was completed. On the second time, immediately going under the water, I heard what I could only describe as the literal sound of death and my body leaving and staying buried under that water. It was intense. It was as if I could see my body dead, having drowned in that water. It was an immediate open vision with dramatic sound effects. That man who went into the water was gone!

It was January. Stepping into the water, it was extremely cold in the natural. Suddenly, the water was hot, intensely hot as if on fire. I felt something grab my right calf. I tried to shake it but it would not fall off.

After the seventh time, the glory and power of God infused my life in a new dimension. It was a deeply personal experience—taking place in public. The young lady taking pictures was frantic. She saw what we could not see. Inches away from us the entire time was a huge shark.

As God called me into this demonstration of obedience, a very real shark circled in the water right where we stood. Michael said he had never seen a shark in the waters there in the multiple times he had been to that beach. When we stood in the sand and looked out, there it was. It not only was a large shark you could see with your natural eyes, it *stayed* there, circling around only in the area exactly where we had been standing. There was no question that being branded by Jesus is a gateway into supernatural power to overcome every scheme and vicious attack of the enemy. God's supernatural protection from this literal shark marked our lives.

We are called to be burning ones. We are torches that are to *run* into the darkest places in our generation and demonstrate the power of Jesus' name in signs, wonders, and miracles. This was a powerful sign and wonder right in front of our eyes. Soon a fish began to jump in and out of the water exactly and only in the area where we had been standing. It was amazing in every dimension!

ANOINTING

I sat on the sand and continued to worship Jesus. His precious presence was so close. The tears flowed. Jesus spoke and told me He wanted to take me somewhere. In my spirit, I told Him I was willing to go. His directive was clear. Ask Michael to anoint me with oil and lay hands on me and He would take me.

I could hardly speak. I looked up at Michael who was to my left, sitting in the sand, and I tried to speak. I motioned with my hand for him to come over. When he knelt next to me, I was able to say, "Jesus wants to take me somewhere. Jesus has instructed me to request that you would anoint me with oil and lay hands on me."

This partnership in the Spirit *must not* be missed. So many ministers of the Gospel are *not* living the life God has called them to directly because they insist on doing life and ministry alone. Their self-built walls are miles high around their heart. They speak the language of brotherhood but refuse to lay down their lives for another. They speak of love for Jesus but are unwilling to sit with Him for hours and gaze into His beautiful face and adore the One who gave His everything for them.

Michael placed oil on his hands. I could feel the strength of his hands. It was Jesus Himself laying His hands on me. I could hear him praying; however, I also felt myself leaving. My body was no longer able to remain upright. Suddenly, I was lying flat out in the sand on that shoreline. I left on my journey with Jesus!

Forty minutes later I shot straight up. Michael informed me that this experience started at exactly 8:00 a.m. He had been watching over me and knew the exact time.

What happened during those forty minutes? I traveled with Jesus in open visions. Jesus took me to Tehran, Iran. I knew where we were when I saw the city monument. He walked me into a prison there. I saw the men, broken in spirit, dressed in what looked like pajamas. One was being severely whipped. I saw his back. I could feel the pain.

Stop the frantic running that masks the emptiness inside. Stop talking. Listen to Him. His presence is transforming you.

When Jesus came to Saul, He declared that He was Jesus whom Saul was persecuting. The love of Jesus for those suffering for His name is beyond what any mortal can articulate. When we strike the followers of Jesus, we strike Jesus Himself. He walked with me through the marketplace.

He spoke to me about the future of my family. There are secrets that Jesus speaks to us that are not to be unveiled. He called for me to come up higher. He spoke to me of how John was in the Spirit on the Lord's Day. He spoke powerfully that He was the one who brought me to that shoreline to anoint, ordain, and commission me. He called me to follow Him just like He called James and John by the water.

This is *your* moment. Rip off everything you have been covering yourself with and be vulnerable, completely vulnerable before God. Let Him take you into Himself. Sit with Him. Stop the frantic running that masks the emptiness inside. Stop talking. Listen to Him. His presence is transforming you. His fire is burning and He is ready to brand you in the deepest part of your heart. Immediately obey His directives. Run into His arms and let Him embrace you. Hold you. Love you. It's *your* time!

I am branded. I will bear in my body the scars of Jesus. Jesus laid down His life for me. I will serve Him with all of my being no matter the cost. I am His laid-down lover. The Lamb that was slain is worthy to receive the *reward* of His sacrifice. Every nation will bow in worship before Him. My greatest desire, my only desire is Jesus Himself.

Christ was marked for me. Throughout all of eternity, Jesus is branded on His hands and feet with the marks of unconditional love for us. My heart belongs only to Him. We are marked by design. We are His burning ones! Let the passion of His burning heart brand you now!

The author and his family, left to right:
John Z, John, RainyDawn, and Jeremiah.

About the Author

J ohn is husband to RainyDawn and father to his two amazing sons, John Z and Jeremiah. At the age of eleven, John had a life-transforming encounter with the Holy Spirit. At age sixteen, while a student in Bible college, he experienced visions that forever marked his life. He currently serves as lead pastor of a thriving international church in New York City.

John and his family are active partners with Burning Ones, the dynamic ministry led by Michael and Anna Dow. John is a laid-down lover of Jesus who burns with passion for Him. John lives to preach the Gospel of the Kingdom where the name of Jesus has never been heard.

Twitter: @jblondonyc

About Burning Ones

By Michael Dow

Burning Ones is the ministry of Michael and Anna Dow. Our vision is to raise up burning ones that will make Jesus famous among the nations of the world. We do that by preaching the Gospel of the Kingdom until the hearts of men and women come alive to God and burn with passion for His Son, Jesus, by the power of the Holy Spirit. We preach Jesus in church services, conferences, and mass crusades around the world with extraordinary signs and miracles.

When He consumes our lives, we become His burning ones! We are burning ones by experience and expression. We experience Him and then we express Him to the world. Burning Ones is not something that is exclusive for us to a specific time and space; it is life itself!

Website: www.burningones.org
Facebook: burningonesinternational
E-mail: info@burningones.org

BOOKS BY MICHAEL DOW

FREE INDEED

Does God have to have your agreement in order for Him to have your obedience? Will you obey the call of God even if there is not an instant payout or benefit to you? Many are willing to step into obedience and do what God is asking so long as they are the primary beneficiaries of their obedience. Are you willing to walk with a God that you cannot control? Can you handle walking with a Jesus that you cannot manipulate and leverage your faithfulness against? There is a confrontation that awaits you in the text...a confrontation to determine what kind of Jesus follower you are going to be. In the book *Free Indeed*, Michael challenges the reader to surrender everything to Jesus and invest the rest of their life into uncompromised obedience to Him.

THE BREAKING POINT

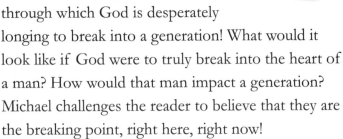

Every generation God seeks after a man or a woman that He can use to partner with Him in changing the world. Our lives are the point through which God is desperately longing to break into a generation! What would it look like if God were to truly break into the heart of a man? How would that man impact a generation? Michael challenges the reader to believe that they are the breaking point, right here, right now!

Books available at:

Amazon
Kindle
iBooks
www.burningones.org